Making Schools
SMARTER

SECOND EDITION

Making Schools SMARTER

A System for Monitoring
School and District Progress

Kenneth Leithwood

Robert Aitken

Doris Jantzi

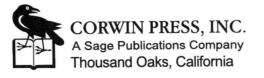

CORWIN PRESS, INC.
A Sage Publications Company
Thousand Oaks, California

For information:

CORWIN PRESS

Corwin Press, Inc.
A Sage Publications Company
2455 Teller Road
Thousand Oaks, California 91320
E-mail: order@corwinpress.com

Sage Publications Ltd.
6 Bonhill Street
London EC2A 4PU
United Kingdom

Sage Publications India Pvt. Ltd.
M-32 Market
Greater Kailash I
New Delhi 110 048 India

Printed in the United States of America

Library of Congress Cataloging-in-Publication Data

Leithwood, Kenneth A.
    Making schools smarter: A system for monitoring school and district progress
    by Kenneth Leithwood, Robert Aitken, and Doris Jantzi.— 2nd ed.
        p. cm.
    Includes bibliographical references (p.) and index.
    ISBN 0-7619-7504-7 (cloth: alk. paper)
    ISBN 0-7619-7505-5 (pbk.: alk. paper)
    1. Educational evaluation—United States. 2. Educational indicators—United States.
    3. Educational accountability—United States. 4. School districts—United States—Evaluation.

    LB2822 .75 .L45 2000
    379.1′58—dc21   00-029536

This book is printed on acid-free paper.

01 02 03 04 05 10 9 8 7 6 5 4 3 2 1

Editorial Assistant: Kylie Liegl
Production Editor: Diana E. Axelsen
Cover Designer: Tracy E. Miller

Contents

Preface

Making Schools Smarter: A System for Monitoring School and District Progress is a practical tool for helping to solve three of the problems most central to school leadership. The first problem is to determine a defensible and compelling image of future schools and districts. Such an image provides a framework for decisions—decisions about immediate goals and priorities, and decisions about the capacities to be developed among staff, for example. *Making Schools Smarter* addresses the problem by offering a relatively comprehensive and detailed image of future schools and districts conceived of as "learning organizations."

Second, *Making Schools Smarter* highlights those aspects of one's organization where changes are most needed if progress toward a valued future image is to be made. It provides not only detailed indicators of learning organizations but also specific techniques and instruments for assessing the extent to which schools and districts reflect these indicators.

Finally, because school leaders are being pressed as never before to be "accountable," *Making Schools Smarter* provides leaders with the tools to demonstrate and improve on their accountability. This is not an easy task. Although obviously a critical element, evidence of student learning alone, for example, will not solve the problem because so many factors outside the control of schools and districts influence such learning. What school organizations can control and therefore be held accountable for is the use of best practices (e.g., instructional practices, administrative practices) and the development of organizations that foster the development of such practices. This second edition of the book reflects our experiences in working with many superintendents and principals over the past four years to use the instruments and procedures outlined in the book to improve their organizations.

OVERVIEW OF CONTENTS

Chapter 1 provides the reader with a synopsis of the school and district monitoring system, the evidence on which it is based, and the assumptions that lie behind it. Chapters 2 and 3 extend the argument, begun in the first chapter, for conceiving of an ideal school and district as a learning organization. These chapters clarify a number of features important to an understanding of the monitoring system. Chapters 4 through 9 describe the core of the monitoring system: the indicators and illustrative measures of those specific features of the model school and district. Inputs are described in Chapter 4, Outcomes in Chapter 5, and District and School Processes in Chapters 6 through 9. Chapter 10 provides some basic information about the application and interpretation of the survey instruments included in Appendixes A and B for the monitoring system for schools and districts, respectively. Guidelines for ensuring productive use of monitoring information are included in the concluding chapter (11).

AUDIENCE

The concepts and tools available in this book are intended primarily for district and school leaders. In addition, however, developers of indicator systems, evaluation specialists, and policymakers ought to find the contents helpful.

ACKNOWLEDGMENTS

The project that gave rise to this book was supported through funds provided by the British Columbia Ministry of Education. In this respect, we are particularly grateful for the support of Sam Lim, Assistant Deputy Minister; and Tom Bennett, Assistant Director, Research and Evaluation.

Administrators and teachers in several school districts made important contributions to the project. Special appreciation is due to the staff of the Greater Victoria School District. Significant contributions were also made by staff from the Kamloops School District.

The authors also acknowledge the psychometric advice and assistance provided by Dr. John Anderson, Chair of Psychological Foundations in Education at the University of Victoria.

The authors wish to especially acknowledge the very large contribution to the project of Karen Henderson, System Applications Specialist, who was responsible for preparing the original manuscript and for developing the design for the survey instruments.

Corwin Press would like to acknowledge the following reviewers:

Michael Cohen
Phoenixville Area School District
Phoenixville, PA

Carol Spencer
Best Practice Designs
Addison, VT

Penelope W. Swenson
Mojave Unified School District
Mojave, CA

Joseph A. Waler
Trinity High School
Garfield Heights, OH

About the Authors

Kenneth Leithwood is Professor of Educational Administration and Head, Centre for Leadership Development at the Ontario Institute for Studies in Education, University of Toronto. He has done research and written extensively on school and district leadership, expert problem-solving processes among leaders, and school improvement processes.

Robert Aitken was, until recently, Director of Planning and Evaluation for the Greater Victoria School District. He has been a teacher, administrator, and Ministry of Education official and is now a private consultant.

Doris Jantzi is a senior research officer with the Centre for Leadership Development at the Ontario Institute for Studies in Education, University of Toronto.

Chapter 1

Introduction

Anecdote 1 (An urgent need for an improvement focus)

The principal of Littlewood Heights Middle School received her students' scores on the state's math and language achievement tests the week before the results of all schools in her district and state were reported in the local paper. Students at Littlewood scored in the lowest 10 percent of middle schools in the state. Among the other six middle schools in the district, Littlewood results were second from the bottom. Littlewood staff are depressed by the results and the reactions to the results by some parents. The principal is experiencing not-so-subtle pressure from the superintendent to provide him with a plan for improving the results. But neither the staff nor the principal has any clear idea of where to begin.

Anecdote 2 (A case of shriveling commitment)

For the past five years, administrators and teachers in School District #101 have been "implementing the state's policies and directions." Primary teachers in the district were strong advocates of the Primary curriculum framework when it first appeared. They even liked the idea of dual entry before the state withdrew it as a component of the framework! Most intermediate staffs in elementary schools embraced the Intermediate framework just as enthusiastically, and several secondary staffs have been experimenting with initiatives likely to be consistent with the senior division framework. In the past year, however, enthusiasm has begun to wane noticeably. More complaints are being voiced by principals, for example, about district budgeting processes that get in the way of their change efforts and district testing policies that send confusing messages to teachers about curriculum priorities. Some parents have also expressed confusion about the gap they see between the role they expect to play in their children's education and the distance with which they are held by the staff of their local school. The superintendent is beginning to ask: "Why is this effort starting to go off the rails? Where should we direct our energies to restore the earlier levels of commitment to the state's initiatives?"

A FIRST PASS AT PURPOSES

Two anecdotes (only slightly fictionalized) illustrate some of the most important purposes the school and district monitoring system is intended to serve.

The questions raised in these two anecdotes are being asked in many parts of the country. Indeed, comparable questions are posed daily within most educational jurisdictions throughout North America. Moreover, lack of good information will prevent the development of productive responses to such questions. The monitoring system was developed in order to provide such information.

Strategic planning, increased accountability, and school restructuring have two things in common. First, they are well-intentioned initiatives, often carried out in ways that actually exacerbate the problems they are intended to solve (examples of what Sieber [1981] referred to as "fatal remedies"). Second, to accomplish their intentions almost always requires more and different kinds of information than schools and districts possess: In many instances, this lack of information accounts for the fatal nature of the remedies, which of course wastes enormous amounts of time, energy, goodwill, public support, and money.

Districts and schools often engage in strategic or school improvement planning as a means of sharpening their priorities in times of fiscal constraint, and to help adapt proactively to internal and external pressures for change. Strategic planning also is viewed as a way to build commitment among organizational members to a shared vision for the future. In many districts and schools, however, the real consequences of strategic planning are altogether different: unmanageably large numbers of "priorities" are identified; so much turbulence is created in the organization's environment that well-targeted improvements become impossible to make; and initial increases in commitment to the organization's directions are followed by pessimism and disillusionment as the school or district finds it impossible to follow through on much of its plan. Any wonder that the title of Henry Mintzberg's recent (1993) book is *The Rise and Fall of Strategic Planning.*

Increased demands on schools to become more accountable typically spring from legitimate concerns that students may not be learning what they should or as much as they ought to learn, and/or that school personnel are not efficient in their practices. But the consequences of tightening the accountability "screws" often are a narrowing and trivializing of the school curriculum and the creation of work cultures that reduce rather than increase professional commitments and circumscribe the full use of existing teacher and administrator capacities.

As a response to the failed school reform efforts of the past, restructuring initiatives aim at fostering substantially more than just "first-order" changes—changes in the services provided directly to students, largely through the school's curriculum and instruction. Restructuring aims also at "second-order" changes—changes in the structures, policies, norms, and the like that either support or detract from the services provided directly to students. Unfortunately, many of the more popular second-order changes now being implemented in schools seem to have little impact on changes in curriculum and instruction. The means for accomplishing many of the student outcomes aspired to by advocates of restructuring are unusually complex, often uncertain and sometimes unknown. The professional learning required for successful restructuring depends on a commitment to experimentation and innovation at the local level.

What types of information would help avoid these unwanted consequences? In many cases, this would include systematically collected information about how well the current status of those elements of the school and district with the greatest impact on students compares with knowledge of best practices. Such information reduces competition among planning participants (engendered by popular procedures for strategic planning) for attention to their "favorite" problem—a competition normally adjudicated by adding everybody's favorite to the list. The negative consequences of increased accountability demands are ameliorated by information about a broader set of indicators of the organization's well-being than is typical of existing indicator systems or the student achievement data collected by many schools and districts. Finally, the local learning required for successful restructuring is aided by feedback about the consequences of innovative practices and information about remaining obstacles to change.

Making Schools Smarter is a monitoring system designed to help schools and districts acquire the information they need to better realize their intentions for improvement, accountability, and school restructuring. In the remainder of this book, you will find a description of an ideal but achievable school and district in the intermediate future (5 to 10 years hence); also included are indicators of specific features of that school and district, and ways of measuring comparable features of current schools and districts. Guidelines are provided for using data generated by such measures to help move current schools and districts closer to the ideal. Because this ideal, as described in the next two chapters, is a "learning organization," movement toward the ideal means that schools and districts will be getting smarter—literally; they will be enhancing their collective capacities to serve students better.

This chapter describes more fully the uses for the monitoring system, summarizes its features, and offers reasons for the choices made in its design. The chapter ends with an overview of the remainder of the book.

THE BIG PICTURE

The monitoring system is selectively comprehensive: selective in its focus only on elements of district and school organizations for which there is convincing evidence of "value-addedness" or impact on important out-comes; comprehensive in its consideration not only of the inputs or resources schools and districts are given to work with (e.g., money) and the outcomes of that work (e.g., student achievement), but also the processes most likely to foster those outcomes (e.g., teaching, leadership).

Figure 1.1 identifies the five dimensions or categories within which are located the more detailed characteristics of the model school and district on which the monitoring system is based. The meaning of these categories is as follows:

Inputs: *Resources available to the school and district, selected characteristics of people served by and employed in the school and district, and the nature of the wider social and cultural context of the community within which the school and district are located. Some inputs are relatively fixed or hard to alter; others may be altered through intentional intervention by those in the district and school.*

District Characteristics, Conditions, and Processes: *Features of the school district believed to make either a direct or indirect contribution to accomplishing desired (immediate and/or long-term) outcomes.*

School Characteristics, Conditions, and Processes: *Features of the school organization believed to make either a direct or indirect contribution to accomplishing desired (immediate and/or long-term) outcomes.*

Immediate Outcomes: *The intended contributions by the district and school to the socioemotional and intellectual growth of individual students as well as to the student population as a whole.*

Long-Term Outcomes: *The intended educational and vocational opportunities and dispositions created for and in students as a consequence of accomplishing immediate outcomes, as well as contributions by the school and district to the social and economic well-being of the broader community within which they are situated.*

WE HAD OUR REASONS

It is important to note that the monitoring system does not specify what the intermediate or long-term outcomes should be. This is a matter of local policy. The monitoring system can be used with any reasonable choice of educational outcomes.

In this section, we review five issues typically considered central in the development of a defensible monitoring system. Responses provided to these issues are intended as an explanation, if not justification, for the choices made in designing the model school and district portrayed in Figure 1.1 as well as the monitoring system developed from it. The issues include:

FIGURE 1.1. Specific Characteristics Included in the Model School and District

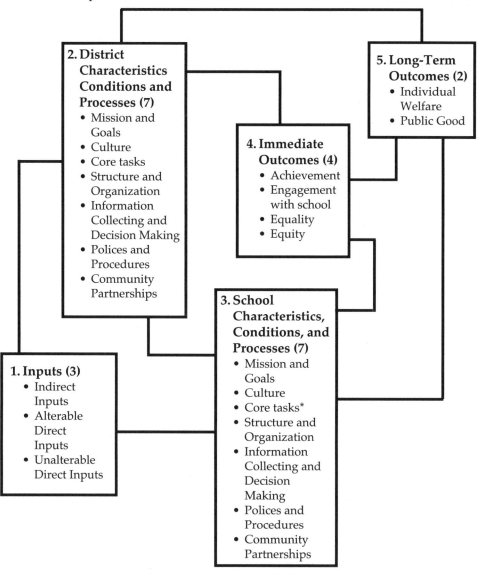

NOTE: This figure identifies the specific qualities or characteristics found within five dimensions of the model school and district. Plausible relationships among the five dimensions are also shown. A more detailed justification and description of these qualities or characteristics is left to subsequent chapters, at which point related indicators and measures also are identified.

* "Core tasks" includes leadership, management, planning, and instruction.

1. **What is a school and district monitoring system, and what purposes should it serve?**

2. **Why should a monitoring system include district and school processes?**

3. **How are elements of the monitoring system related?**

4. **How detailed should a monitoring system be?**

5. **How can a monitoring system be future oriented?**

What Is a School and District Monitoring System and What Purposes Should It Serve?

The ultimate long term test of this system is not whether we are better informed but whether we act more prudently.
(Bryk & Hermanson, 1993, p. 476)

A monitoring system is a concise description of what should be and a process to determine what is. What this means can be explained more fully by comparing a monitoring system with an education indicator system. In Oakes's terms, an indicator system is "a statistic about the educational system that reveals something about its performance or health" (1986, p. 1). A set or system of indicators is an accumulation of such statistics. We view a monitoring system as a framework within which to select or define, interpret, and use a wide array of indicators. *The central distinction between a system of indicators and a monitoring system is the requirement, in the case of a monitoring system, that regularly collected information be translated into courses of action. These courses of action will usually be informed by the strategic directions established by the school and district.* To serve this purpose, then, a monitoring system must be based on a coherent understanding of what is being monitored. In contrast, an indicator system requires no such understanding.

Although all monitoring systems collect information, evaluate it, and initiate action as a result, the nature of the action will differ considerably depending upon one's assumptions about the nature of the organization being monitored. As discussed further in Chapter 2, there are several alternatives. If one assumes the organization to be a bureaucracy, the information most certainly will be used (often by those in central positions) to diagnose deviations from policy, to determine organizational strengths and weaknesses in accomplishing specific goals, and then to launch remedial action. We refer to this as *centralized, instrumental use* of the monitoring information. A monitoring system is, in a bureaucracy, a management information system.

Some people, however, prefer to think of schools and districts as communities. From this view, the value of the information provided by the monitoring system is *individual enlightenment*; such information aims "to change the basic ideas that ground day-to-day life in schools" (Bryk & Hermanson, 1993, p. 454). There may be no immediate action resulting from this change in basic ideas. But one expects such changes in thinking eventually to influence at least the actions of some individual members of the organization as they come to understand their work differently.

As we will explain in considerably more detail in Chapter 3, however, neither bureaucracies nor communities provide fully satisfactory perspectives on which to premise assumptions about a school or district. More satisfactory, we believe, is a view of the school and district as *a learning organization*—an organization with the collective dispositions and structural characteristics enabling it to learn, through its own and others' experiences, how to continuously "get better," to behave more "intelligently." When conceived of in such terms, a monitoring system ought to serve as a powerful stimulus for raising the organization's collective capacities. Most certainly this will require enlightenment—changes in basic ideas and understandings. Not just enlightenment of individuals, however, but of teams engaged in collective problem solving, as well. And most certainly such enlightenment will lead to instrumental action by both individuals and teams. Such action may include remediating organizational weaknesses in relation to existing goals, what Argyris and Schön (1978) refer to as "single-loop learning." But it will sometimes also include redefining such goals and rethinking the norms, values, and beliefs on which are based organizational policies and practices (double-loop learning).

Monitoring systems, then, serve learning organizations by fostering both single- *and* double-loop learning. Such learning needs to occur at the small-group or team level, at the school level, and at the central district level. In principle, the monitoring system and the information it produces have relevance for every individual or group with a stake in the quality of the school's or district's work. For a learning organization, a monitoring system is a vehicle through which mostly small incremental additions (but occasionally large, radical changes) can be made to the collective capacities of its members. A monitoring system allows this to happen to the extent that the potential users of the information it provides have developed habits of collective reflection and consequent action to which information from the monitoring system can be introduced.

There are at least five important reasons why district and school processes ought to feature prominently in a district monitoring system, if not an indicator system, as well.

Why Should a Monitoring System Include District and School Processes?

Processes Are Ends in Their Own Right. There can be no doubt that educators, parents, and the public-at-large worry about how successfully schools assist students in accomplishing what the monitoring system refers to as **Outcomes**. By no stretch of the imagination, however, is that all they worry about; it is not the case

School is not just preparation for life after school, it *is* life.

that any "means" are justified if such "ends" are accomplished. As a minimum, these "means" of education, most of us insist, must be humane. Furthermore, we hope they are pleasant from the students' point of view, even exciting, engaging, and compelling. After all, school is not just preparation for life after school, it *is* life; for those who graduate from secondary school, the experience figures prominently throughout 15% to 20% of the total years of their lives. That is a long time in which to be bored, frustrated, and unhappy, even if one does leave the experience literate and numerate.

Equity Goals Demand Process Measures. As evidence has accumulated in response to education's equity agenda, it has become shockingly clear that the quality and extent of school processes are often distributed among students quite unevenly. For example, students who find themselves in the non-academic streams or tracks of some secondary schools often experience less talented teachers, poorer quality instruction, "watered-down" curricula, and more restrictive learning environments. Equity means, among other things, equal access to the same quality and quantity of educational resources (or processes). Aggregated outcome measures cannot detect inequity. Input-output analyses usually point to the student's socioeconomic status as the "explanation" for a large proportion of variation in outcomes among students. One needs information about school processes, however, to pinpoint what it is that schools actually do, or don't do, to alter the predictable effects of SES (socioeconomic status) inputs. If all that schools do is exacerbate or reproduce the inequities kids bring with them to their school experience, we can hardly claim to be addressing problems of inequity.

... even though we do not fully understand how schools produce the results we want, context information may provide clues ... about why we get the outcomes we do.
(Oakes, 1989, p. 182)

Process Measures Offer Clues to School Improvement. This is an entirely instrumental reason for including process measures in a school and district monitoring system. Just consider what you don't know when all that are measured are inputs and outputs and when the outputs seem unsatisfactory. You don't know why—not a clue. So process measures offer clues. They pinpoint features of the district's or school's functioning that might help explain disappointing outcomes allowing one to orient efforts to change around those features.

It is difficult to overemphasize the importance of process measures for this purpose. Even though their value seems self-evident, policy groups everywhere persist in measuring outcomes in as technically rigorous a manner as possible but basing recommendations for change on almost no systematic data whatever. The result? Wave after wave of solutions to the wrong problems. Or the bizarre strategy of increasing the testing of outcomes even more based on the expectations that this will somehow, magically, improve them. This is something to do when you don't know what to do, a declaration of intellectual bankruptcy.

Process Measures Balance the Effects of Technical Shortcomings. Only a small range of the outcomes we aspire to for students can actually be measured, at least on a very large scale, in a technically adequate and cost-feasible manner. Simple skills and factual knowledge—easy; complex problem-solving skills— harder; capacities for aesthetic appreciation, development of self-direction in learning, mathematical creativity, persistence, realistic self-concept—nope, no time soon.

We are painfully aware, however, of what happens when the only outcomes measured are the ones that can be measured well.

We are painfully aware, however, of what happens when the only outcomes measured are that can be measured well. The ubiquitous curriculum steering effect sets in. If the results of the measurement actually count for something, especially if they are somehow seen to be "high stakes," the curriculum that is taught quickly begins to approximate the curriculum that is tested. In the face of such a consequence, measures of school and district processes symbolically announce that other outcomes matter, that the outcomes not directly measured but expected to develop through measured processes also deserve attention.

Such measurement does have symbolic value. But that is not all. It is indirect evidence of what is being learned, as well, since what is taught is usually a powerful predictor of what is learned.

Process Measures Monitor Restructuring Initiatives. Many reform efforts, certainly those embodied in many state and provincial restructuring initiatives, advocate changing the nature of the curriculum, types of classroom instruction, the organization of students, assessment, reporting of student progress, and the like. These are all processes carried out in the school and classroom. Other initiatives such as decentralized decision making and altered governance structures imply changed district processes. Including process measures in the monitoring system provides direct information about the progress being made in implementing reform.

Although this remains a controversial matter, process measures are actually a far more defensible basis for demonstrating a school or district's accountability than are outcome measures. It is these processes over which educators have control. It is reasonable, therefore, to expect that teachers and administrators will implement those processes judged to be most effective by themselves, policymakers, the profession, and the research community. Also reasonable is the expectation that such processes will be implemented with discretion and that educators will refine them and develop better processes in a continuous effort to improve their practices. Having met all of these expectations, however, a school or district may still "produce" outcomes that someone or many people consider unsatisfactory. Educators have no control over this because such outcomes are also a product of many influences other than the students' school experiences: the aptitudes they bring to the school, the family's educational culture, and the norms and attitudes pervasive in the wider community, for example. Also, educators rarely have any control over the standard against which achieved outcomes are compared. Such standards often vary widely among those who respond to reports of the results of student achievement testing.

These limitations on the accountability of educators parallel limitations on almost all professions, although in many other professions these limitations seem to be better appreciated. Medical practitioners, for example, are expected to skillfully use the best available healing and surgical techniques with discretion; their patients still die, sooner or later, without the doctor being blamed. A greater emphasis on process measures as part of a monitoring system may assist in shifting the basis for educational accountability onto more defensible grounds. This is not likely to happen if the only

Educators rarely have any control over the standard against which achieved outcomes are compared.

evidence reported to the public is about student achievement, although that is obviously one important type of evidence to report.

It is tempting to read Figure 1.1 as though relationships among the five dimensions of the model school district joined by lines were causal in nature, with the direction of causality moving from left to right. Indeed, this was how we ourselves thought of the relationships in the early stages of developing the monitoring system. Furthermore, there may remain some reasons for assuming that is the nature of the relationships even yet. For example, the use of causal modeling techniques to analyze quantitative data collected about the five aggregate dimensions of the monitoring system likely would require some version of this assumption.

However, as the specific characteristics of each dimension are considered, the assumption of a simple, one-way flow of cause and effects quickly becomes untenable. For example, consider the relationship between **Inputs** and **District Characteristics**. Financial resources (an input) have an obvious effect on policies and procedures. You cannot set a pupil-teacher ratio of 15 to 1 in district classrooms unless you have an exceptional district budget. On the other hand, the district can introduce procedures for altering its financial resources—holding a district referendum, for example. Causal relationships become even harder to imagine as one considers elements within dimensions. For example, do the mission and goals of the school determine the school's culture, or is it more likely the other way around? Or is it reciprocal?

These puzzles have led Bryk and Hermanson (1993) to caution: "Beware the causal (sic) modeler" (p. 471). They explain that

> *What we know in a rigorous scientific sense is limited by extant research technology. The linear additive, unidirectional models that are the stock in trade of the quantitative social scientist are far too simplistic a representation for the phenomena under study. No analyst, if really pressed, is likely to maintain that social reality is a simple ensemble of non-interacting additive components. (p. 461)*

Having raised the caution, however, Bryk and Hermanson still recommend that monitoring systems have a strong conceptual organization, one that faithfully reflects those causal relationships that are apparent in

How Are Elements of the Monitoring System Related?

There are only four possible things that can happen among events in an organization. The events can be either similar or different, and they can occur either at the same or at different times.
(Weick & Bougon, 1986, p. 103)

available research and "the best clinical expertise" (p. 468). Oakes (1989) argues for the consideration of such relationships as "enabling"—a kind of soft causality. This is, we think, a sensible view of the relationships evident among the five major dimensions of the model school district. But we offer no advice on the relationship among the specific characteristics within each dimension of the monitoring system.

How Detailed Should a Monitoring System Be?

During its development, the single most frequently raised concern about the monitoring system was its detail or comprehensiveness. **"It has to be much simpler to be understood,"** we were advised. **"Too much information will be overwhelming,"** people argued, **"and make it impossible to determine priorities for action." "What is needed,"** our advisors said, **"is good information about a small, manageable number of key indicators."**

Your car could have gauges describing every system and function within it, but it does not. . . . You assume that if a wheel bearing wears out, you will hear it.
(Selden, 1990, p. 386)

This is good advice about an issue that has plagued most other efforts to build educational monitoring and indicator systems. In their extensive review of such efforts, Bryk and Hermanson (1993) note that a complete model of a school system lies far beyond our current knowledge: "Such knowledge is partial and does not approach an integrated theory of school organization, processes and effects" (p. 462). They also concur, however, with the position we took in response to our advisors. Our position was to develop as detailed a model of schools and districts as evidence permitted and as we thought the purposes for the monitoring system demanded. This meant a substantially more detailed monitoring system than some of our advisors had in mind. But pinpointing the district and school processes plausibly accounting for achieved outcomes, a key purpose for the monitoring system, seemed to demand nothing less. Of course, the system may indeed be overly complex and unwieldy for other purposes. Using selected elements of the system piecemeal may be quite suitable for these other purposes.

How Can a Monitoring System Be Future Oriented?

Let's start by asking why the monitoring system ought to be future oriented, in case that is not yet clear. The short answer is that its purposes require a future orientation. As the main justification offered for including district and school processes, we argued that central to the purpose for monitoring was the pinpointing of reasons for the accomplishment and non-accomplishment of important outcomes. It is possible to construe this purpose as serving to maintain the school or district in a stable state or condition of equilibrium; this would be somewhat analogous to the diagnostic-remedial model of medical practice aimed at maintaining bodily health. But we pointed out also that the actions in response to such diagnostic clues about the organization's health were to be generated within the framework of the organization's strategic decisions.

This point deserves more attention than it has received so far because it was central to the motivation for developing the monitoring system. After investing considerable effort in strategic planning and the early stages of pursuing the directions established through such planning, many schools and districts began to look for a systematic means of assessing their progress and making mid-course adjustments. No strategic plan is needed for standing still (a plan perhaps, but not a "strategic" plan). So strategic planning efforts signal a commitment to change. In fact, the content of such plans often indicate a commitment to some quite substantial organizational restructuring. The monitoring system helps meet this commitment by being future oriented.

That's our answer to the *why* question. On to the *how* question. How can a monitoring system be future oriented? Our answer lies in the nature of the information on which the district and school processes parts of the system are built and on what uses are made of that information. Four types of information were considered. The first was the literature reviewed in Chapter 3 about the nature of a learning organization; in particular the conditions within an organization that foster organizational learning. A second type was research aimed at describing effective classrooms, schools, and districts. A selected set of original studies and broad reviews of this research, which we believed to be of good quality, were included. The pool of research encompassed by this category is vast but uneven; an extensive corpus of research has been generated about classroom and teaching effectiveness, less (but still substantial amounts) on school effectiveness, and very modest amounts on district effectiveness. Good representatives of research results from this literature can be found, for example, in Reynolds (1989) on teacher and classroom effectiveness, in Stringfield and Herman (1996) on school effectiveness, and in Leithwood (1995) on district effectiveness.

Research flying the "effectiveness" banner, however, has a distinctive character no matter which level of the school system it concerns. For example, it tends to focus on a narrow and traditional set of student

To choose a direction [members of an organization] must first have developed a mental image of a possible and desirable future state of the organization. This vision ... articulates a view of a realistic, credible, attractive future for the organization, a condition that is better in some important ways than what now exists.
(Bennis & Nanus, 1985, p. 89)

outcomes as the basis for judging effectiveness. It does not call into question the basic characteristics of existing schools, taking them, rather, as givens; it promotes a relatively aggressive and directive image of school leadership; and it is premised on assumptions about school organizations as bureaucracies.

This literature can only be considered future oriented in a very narrow sense. For schools in troubled environments, serving many students from disadvantaged backgrounds and experiencing difficulty helping those students to meet minimum, basic educational expectations, this literature describes what has worked for some schools and what might work for others. It is a literature that depicts a modest but worthwhile short-term future for schools faced with a particular set of narrowly proscribed but difficult problems.

A third type of literature on which the monitoring system was based concerns the reengineering and "restructuring" of organizations, both school and non-school organizations. This is a quickly growing body of literature heavily weighted with provocative suggestions for change, sensitive to the general trend toward the democratization of social institutions worldwide, and centrally premised on assumptions about individual empowerment. Its empirical grounding is, as yet, quite weak, as compared with the literature on teacher effectiveness, for example. The distinctive characteristic of this body of literature, when it considers schools, is to focus on a broad, ambitious, and nontraditional set of student outcomes; its questioning of traditional school social structures; and its promotion of facilitative and transformational forms of leadership. Consistent with directions evident in many leading-edge, non-school organizations, this literature assumes that bureaucracy is anathema to progress and is to be replaced by more community-like social structures.

Prototypical of this literature in education are the concise syntheses provided by Conley (1991) and Murphy (1991). Naisbitt and Aburdene's (1985) *Reinventing the Corporation* is a good representation of the organizational restructuring literature outside of schools. This restructuring literature is clearly future oriented. In its consideration of schools, the effects of many of its key proposals on the growth of students remains to be determined empirically (e.g., site-based management). But for some restructuring advocates that is not an essential link; a more democratic institution is a worthwhile end in itself. The restructuring literature imagines a quite ambitious, intermediate-term future for a broad spectrum of schools.

Finally, we attempted to reflect, in the district monitoring system, the implications for schools of a literature concerned with broad social trends and how to respond to them organizationally. Examples of this category of literature include Schwartz's (1991) *The Art of the Long View* and Senge's (1990) *The Fifth Discipline*. This literature is sometimes quite speculative, but it does offer a significant challenge to single-loop learning and stretches the futures horizon to something more distant than do the other categories of literature reviewed.

We used these four literatures in an effort to model important features of a school and district that would be effective in the present and have the capacity to gradually transform itself into the kind of school and district that would also be effective ten years from now. Use of the monitoring system allows a school and district to compare itself with this model, identifying changes it feels would be useful to make to more fully approximate some aspects of the model school and district it especially values.

We used these four literatures in an effort to model important features of a school and district that would be effective in the present and have the capacity to gradually transform itself into the kind of school and district that would also be effective 10 years from now. ✓

✳ ✳ ✳ ✳ ✳ ✳

SUMMARY

The model on which is based the monitoring system consists of five dimensions: **Inputs** (e.g., family educational culture), **District and School Processes** (e.g., mission and goals, culture), and both **Immediate and Long-Term Outcomes** (e.g., student achievement, preparation for work). A total of 30 specific factors, variables, or elements of the school and district are distributed across these five dimensions. The overall model, as well as its specific features, emerged from a synthesis of theory and research about learning organizations and about effective classrooms, schools, and districts. As well, the model reflects theory and research about educational restructuring and about the future implications for education of broad social trends that currently seem to be of consequence.

Although tempting, the relationships among dimensions and specific features of the model cannot be considered causal. A more realistic description in some cases would be "interactive." Nevertheless, there will be instances of use of the monitoring system in which examining some relationships as causal will make sense. Research evidence about some such relationships is quite robust, but this is not generally the case. Long-term applications of the monitoring system, however, have the potential to teach us more about these relationships.

Because a central purpose for the monitoring system is to pinpoint district and/or school processes that might serve as a focus for change, the model is relatively detailed. Such detail may be unnecessary when the monitoring system is used for other purposes. For example, reporting progress in implementing reforms, accounting to the public for use of resources or providing individual schools with information bearing on specific priorities which they have—these would be purposes that could be well served by using only selected features of the district monitoring system.

Finally, the monitoring system was designed to be used within the framework of an organization's strategic directions. But it is also sensible to expect such directions to emerge out of initial uses of the monitoring system. To the extent that the monitoring system is based on a future-oriented model school and district, evidence of discrepancies between the model and one's own organization is a clear alternative (or supplement) to more conventional methods for goal setting within a strategic or school improvement planning process.

PART I: BASIC ASSUMPTIONS ABOUT SCHOOLS AND DISTRICTS

Aristotelian logic depends on the concept of precise sets: **a statement is either true or false; a person is either a man or a woman; a living organism is either animal or vegetable**. Bureaucratic organizations are largely premised on the same logic. An employee is either a manager or a worker, either a leader or a follower. If this person is a manager then, for example, she makes decisions, is privy to particular information, and has high status; if this person is a worker then she follows directions, is privy to other types of information, and has relatively low status. The boxes and arrows on the conventional organizational chart imply little or no overlap in functions, responsibilities and status among those who occupy the positions designated by the boxes.

Such precision in the classification of positions, functions, and the people attached to them brings with it a comforting sense of certainty and control, especially to those with a low tolerance for ambiguity (and newspaper reporters who ask such questions as, "Is twinning schools a good thing or a bad thing?"). People such as these might even begin to believe that they understand how an organization, framed in these terms, actually works and can be managed. But they would be deluding themselves. Precise sets, of the Aristotelian variety, are almost exclusive to mathematics and classic schools of logic.

The organizational chart has no reality outside the assumptions it gives rise to and these assumptions no longer serve us well.

In the world outside classical logic and mathematics, distinctions between things are much more vague. Decisions are neither good nor bad; almost all courses of action on some occasions could be either. Indeed, beyond the simplest of distinctions, the meaning of good and bad blurs quickly into a quagmire of cultural, moral and situational considerations. Similarly, just to appreciate how organizations actually work requires one to consider individual people and groups in much more dynamic and multidimensional ways than is suggested by the bureaucratically-inspired organizational chart. Redesigning organizations, like schools or districts, so they are capable of responding to the demands which they will face in the near and mid-term future means largely jettisoning the chart altogether. The organizational chart has no reality outside the assumptions it gives rise to and these assumptions no longer serve us well.

Whereas bureaucratic organizations were premised on Aristotelian logic (precise sets), K-12 education systems capable of responding, for example, to restructuring initiatives will be premised on "fuzzy logic." Now "fuzzy logic" is a hazardous term because its common sense meaning implies confused thinking. But it is actually a technical term for a much more sophisticated form of logic than Aristotle ever imagined (McNeil & Freiberger, 1993). This form of logic, which began its development in the 1960s, is now revolutionizing contemporary information processing systems and the myriad of practical applications of such systems. It is also a useful form of logic to use in imagining the nature of non-bureaucratic educational organizations. Such organizations embrace rather than eschew overlapping responsibilities, collective accountability, open-ended tasks, imprecise goals, and evolutionary planning. They do this because, as Lofti Zadeh, the father of fuzzy logic, explains,

The concept of a "learning organization" is used to generate principles for the ideal school and district.

> *As the complexity of a system increases, our ability to make precise yet significant statements about its behavior diminishes until a threshold is reached beyond which precision and significance (or relevance) become almost mutually exclusive characteristics.* (quoted in McNeil & Freiberger, 1993, p. 43)

Lofti's own example to illustrate the point about diminishing precision is check-out time at a hotel. As we all know, it **isn't** one o'clock as the sign on the back of the hotel door pretends.

For those who prefer their ideas dressed in more informal garb, Bolman and Deal (1991) express much the same notion metaphorically:

> *Taking action in an organization is like firing a cue ball into a complex and large array of billiard balls. So many balls bounce off one another in so many directions that it is hard to know if the final outcome will bear any resemblance to what was intended.* (p. 26)

The two chapters in this section of the book explain the basic assumptions on which was developed the model or ideal school and district central to the monitoring system. These assumptions accept overlapping sets and fuzzy logic as a starting point for thinking about such organizations. The concept of a "learning organization" is used to generate principles for the ideal school and district.

Chapter 2

Clarifying Assumptions:
Three Perspectives

The basic assumption one holds about the nature of schools and school districts makes an enormous difference to the character of a monitoring system. Purposes, data collection and analysis procedures, roles of participants, and the uses made of information all will vary depending on this assumption. Accordingly, we take this opportunity to explain some of the most important assumptions on which this monitoring system is based. These are assumptions about what schools and school districts *ought to be like* in order to behave as learning organizations. Of course, some schools and districts already reflect some or all of our assumptions—but they are relatively rare, certainly in the minority. At the same time, we believe our assumptions are realistic. The small number of districts and schools which currently reflect those assumptions support this belief.

The assumptions one makes about what district and school organizations ought to be like depend, to a considerable degree, on what one holds to be their purposes. And on this matter, we believe that the curriculum frameworks and other aspects of many restructuring efforts will prove to be essentially correct: correct in their image of the educated person and the goals of education that will need to be pursued for that image to be realized, and certainly on the right track with respect to the basic principles guiding the development of curriculum and instruction. Of course, no one would claim that the book is closed on these matters and that all related problems have been solved. That will not and ought not ever to be the case. But we do believe that the "first-order" changes called for by many of these initiatives (the goals for students and the direct services provided to help accomplish those goals) are justified by current professional and research-based knowledge about such matters.

First-order changes are almost never successfully institutionalized in the absence of complementary second-order changes.

However, if there has been one single lesson of special value learned from the flood of research about educational change that has washed over us in the past 20 years, it is this: First-order changes are almost never successfully institutionalized in the absence of complementary second-order changes. ("What in the world," you ask, "is a second-order change?" It is a change in the organization of the district; a change, for example, in policy or resources or structure or culture.) Although this lesson seems disarmingly simple in hindsight, it took a lot of failure for us to realize that the organization in place at the time of initiating a change is normally designed to support the status quo—to ensure, in fact, that the status quo perseveres in the face of uncontrollable changes in people and unanticipated outside events. So, for example, teachers' interests in and commitment to implementing more active forms of learning in the classroom (a first-order change), as Gross, Giacquinta, and Bernstein's early (1971) study showed us, were not able to withstand the press toward more teacher-directed forms of instruction rewarded by, among other things, unchanged teacher supervision practices.

Failures such as this help us to appreciate, for example, that "teaching for understanding" (Cohen, McLaughlin, & Talbert, 1993), a key element of many current reform efforts, will require changes that push deeply into the often taken-for-granted fabric of district and school organizations, not just changes in curriculum and instruction.

. . . two of the three organizational arrangements that required changes to make them compatible with the new teacher role model were never altered during the period of implementation and the third, although adjusted to some extent, was still restrictive to a considerable degree.
(Gross et al., 1971, p. 142)

State and provincial restructuring initiatives often do identify some of the second-order changes likely to be needed; closer relationships with parents as partners with schools in the education of their children and revised forms of student assessment, for example. Different forms and additional amounts of staff development have also been provided by districts. And the physical facilities of some schools have been adapted to accommodate new forms of instruction, as well. Making these second-order changes has contributed significantly to the implementation and institutionalization of curriculum and instructional change advocated by advocates of restructuring (e.g., Leithwood et al, 1991, 1992, 1993). Nevertheless, these second-order changes have been piecemeal. They have not grown out of a systematic effort to imagine what a fully restructured school or district ought to be. So we cannot be sure that something important has not been overlooked or that the most crucial changes are being advocated. Only as we raise our sights to the level of the school and district organization, as a whole, are we likely to find a systematic and relatively comprehensive basis from which to identify the second-order changes needed. Only then, we believe, will the full scope of the restructuring task required be evident.

Raising one's sights to the level of the organization, as a means of identifying a comprehensive set of second-order changes, still leaves choices to be made. The primary choices are among competing perspectives on the nature of districts and schools as organizations, perspectives which also suggest very different purposes and procedures for monitoring. What are the alternatives? Bryk and Hermanson (1993) describe two. Schools and districts, they suggest, may be viewed either as "rational bureaucracies" or as "communities". When districts are portrayed as rational bureaucracies, in the foreground of the picture is the functional division of labor among adults, rule-governed social interactions, role-based forms of authority, and administrative practices tied closely to formal policies and procedures. It is assumed that the purpose for organization is to control the actions taken to accomplish predetermined purposes. The primary means for ensuring employee loyalty to the organization are assumed to be extrinsic rewards. District monitoring activities, within this conception of an organization, are assumed to be for the purposes of assisting with control and better holding people accountable for fulfilling role obligations.

Portraying districts and schools as communities, in contrast, highlights a very different set of assumptions. As Bryk and Hermanson (1993) explain (with schools as their focus):

> *The personal-communitarian perspective favors a more diffuse rather than specialized adult role and a minimum division of labor. It emphasizes the informal and enduring social relationships on which teaching and learning draw and the influence of a school's normative environment. . . . While a deference to formal authority is often the explicit mechanism of control, this authority, in turn, rests on a set of shared understandings that order the largely autonomous behavior of school participants. (p. 454)*

McLaughlin's (1992) evidence suggests that a significant portion of teachers' sense of pride and satisfaction with their work can be explained by variation in these community characteristics, as they are manifest at the district level. District monitoring activities, given a community perspective on schools and districts, are assumed not to be for purposes of control but to stimulate changes in organizational members' basic ideas about daily life in schools and districts.

THREE PERSPECTIVES ON SCHOOL DISTRICT ORGANIZATIONS: A FIRST GLIMPSE

Although the rational bureaucracy perspective has dominated under-standings of schools and districts for at least several decades, many educational reform efforts beginning in the 1980s or earlier were premised on much more community-like perspectives. This is evident, for example, in initiatives toward greater site-based management, increased parental involvement in school governance, and greater participation of teachers in school and district decision-making (see Beck & Foster, 1999, for an excellent recent review). Such reflections of community perspectives on educational organizations parallel comparable changes in many private-sector organizations during the same period.

Does this attachment to community-related ideas mean, then, that adopt-ing a community perspective for our purposes is warranted? Not quite. Although bureaucratic perspectives on school organizations miss much that explains variation in their effectiveness, the need for readily visible, formal mechanisms of control and accountability in publiclyfunded insti-tutions is undeniable, indeed much stronger now than when we first wrote the book. Furthermore, although a community perspective usefully draws attention to the heart and mind of the organization (Sergiovanni, 1994), it is simply naive to assume that these critical "organs" can function in the absence of structural support provided by some form of skeletal bureau-cratic system. Furthermore, the accountability legitimately demanded of education institutions by a society with fixed or diminishing resources to distribute for multiple social services makes the community perspectives' emphasis on nurturance and its implicit neglect of "harder" goals (intellec-tual and vocational, for example) problematic. If schools are to survive, they must be seen to be making unique contributions to the welfare of their clients, as well as contributions complementary to the purposes of other social service institutions. This has led us to adopt a third perspective on school and district organizations, which, we believe, avoids the need for the sorts of untenable trade-offs discussed to this point—districts and schools as learning organizations.

> **If schools are to survive, they must be seen to be making unique contributions to the welfare of their clients, as well as contributions complementary to the purposes of other social service institutions.**

THREE PERSPECTIVES ON SCHOOL AND DISTRICT ORGANIZATIONS: A DEEPER LOOK

Tables 2.1 and 2.2 offer a more detailed illustration of how assumptions, reasonably evoked (and we do not claim more than this) by these three perspectives on organizations, compare. One purpose for the more de-tailed comparison is to help further justify the choice of a "learning organization" perspective on schools and districts as the basis on which

TABLE 2.1.   Basic Assumptions About Human Nature Associated With
Three Perspectives on the School and District

Assumptions	School/District as Bureaucracy	School/District as Community	School/District as Learning Organization
1. Sources of Motivation	• emphasize extrinsic sources • focus on meeting lower-level needs (security)	• emphasize intrinsic sources • focus on meeting affiliation needs	• emphasize both intrinsic and extrinsic sources • focus on meeting esteem and self-actualization needs
2. Nature of the Learning Process	• passive learner • behaviorist explanations • depends on contingent rewards	• active learner • developmentalist explanations (effortless) • depends on stimulating environments	• active learner • constructivist explanations (effortful) • depends on individual and social sense making

the monitoring system was designed. A second is to help account for some
of the critical features that were designed into the monitoring system.

Most perspectives on the nature of organizations grow out of important,
although usually implicit, assumptions about human nature—what it is
that motivates people and how they learn. The three perspectives under
consideration here appear to be based on markedly different assumptions
concerning these matters, as is evident in Table 2.1. Evoked by the bureaucracy perspective are assumptions about the importance of such extrinsic
rewards as income, position, benefits, and the like. Using Maslow's (1970)
needs hierarchy, bureaucracies appear to focus most explicitly on meeting
their members' lower level "security" needs. In contrast, a community
perspective is more explicitly focused on intrinsic motivators; in particular, meeting the "affiliation" needs of its members. These are satisfactions
that come from emotional attachments with one's students and adult
colleagues, for example.

Our conception of the learning organization suggests that it, too, addresses
its members' intrinsic sources of motivation. But, wisely, it does not ignore
extrinsic sources. While evidence (e.g., Lortie, 1975) suggests that teachers,
at least, are primarily motivated by intrinsic sources (evidence of growth
among their students, for example), extrinsic sources can have negative
effects when they are perceived as inadequate but cannot be overlooked.

Recent evidence about the implementation of large-scale reform also argues for attention to extrinsic rewards (e.g., Odden, 1996). Furthermore, a learning organization perspective while addressing intrinsic affiliation needs seems likely, as well, to address the higher level intrinsic needs, those that Maslow (1970), for example, referred to as "esteem" needs (e.g., feelings of achievement, recognition by others) and "self-actualization" needs (e.g., professional growth).

Table 2.1 also presents a summary of assumptions about the nature of learning evoked by the three perspectives on organizations. Differences on this matter appear to closely reflect different schools of learning theory that have developed within the field of psychology over the past forty years. The much discredited behaviorist (or Skinnerian) explanation of human learning, premised on schedules of reinforcement for correct behavior and a relatively passive role for learners explains much of what is assumed to go on in bureaucracies. Alternatively, the organization-as-community perspective evokes an effortless or natural (perhaps Piagetian) model of learning, requiring only a stimulating environment for the development of increasingly complex forms of intellectual functioning. Learning organizations evoke assumptions about the learner as an active participant in the process, about learning as requiring effort, and being goal directed: Such learning occurs as people, individually or collectively, make sense of the events, problems and challenges which they encounter. It is a "constructivist" view of learning, supported by a substantial body of recent evidence from the cognitive sciences (e.g., Posner, 1990) and currently the basis for much curriculum reform and instructional innovation. Unquestionably, this is the dominant paradigm for explaining individual human learning at the present time.

Table 2.2 extends the clarification of assumptions underlying the monitoring system by moving from assumptions concerned with human nature to those bearing directly on critical aspects of the organization.

Table 2.2 extends the clarification of assumptions underlying the monitoring system by moving from assumptions concerned with human nature to those bearing directly on critical aspects of the organization. The seven categories within which these assumptions are described (left column) were derived from organizational design theory (e.g., Banner & Gagne, 1995) and from research on effective schools and districts. They are the same categories used in the district monitoring system's description of school and district processes. More justification for using these categories will be provided later in this volume. We will let Table 2.2 speak for itself,

TABLE 2.2. Basic Assumptions About Critical Aspects of Organizations
Associated With Three Perspectives on the School and District

Assumptions	School/District as Bureaucracy	School/District as Community	School/District as Learning Organization
1. Mission and Goals	• excellence • precise, closed-ended	• equity • vague, open-ended	• quality • clear, evolving
2. Culture	• balkanized • norms of individual achievement and competitions	• collegial • norms of caring and good will	• collaborative • norms of continuous problem solving
3. Management and Leadership (Core Tasks)	• transactional, classic • authoritarian, aggressive • positional power	• servant-like • democratic or laissez-faire	• self-management • transformational • facilitative power
4. Structure and Organization	• hierarchical	• flat	• depends on task and context
5. Decision Making	• individual centered • bounded rationality	• group centered • consensus/majority • non-rational	• team centered (synectic) • post rational
6. Policies and Procedures	• extensive • specify responsibilities	• minimal • only those required by legislation	• minimal • designed to enhance learning and avoid limiting the use of talent
7. Relations with Community	• formal • distant • minimally responsive	• informal • seamless • highly responsive	• formal • partnership • highly responsive

to a large extent, describing the assumptions it records only briefly and
with most attention to those concerning learning organizations.

When schools, for example, behave as learning organizations, their members develop a clear and shared understanding of the school's mission and
goals. It is an evolving understanding, to be sure, but at most points in time
there is little confusion about purposes. And whatever the specific goals
might be, the school's overall mission is to constantly improve the quality
of the services it provides to all of its students and broader community. This
is preferable to equity or excellence as overall missions with typical trade-
offs that disadvantage one or other groups of school clients.

**When schools behave as
learning organizations, their
members develop a clear and
shared understanding of the
school's mission and goals.**

The learning organization's culture is truly collaborative. Members contribute to one another's learning as they address non-routine problems of quality improvement. Such a culture is considerably more than just collegial, a culture in which people display good will toward one another but rarely problem solve together in a systematic way. Balkanized cultures, to use Hargreaves and Macmillan's (1991) distinction, in which collaboration is carried out only at the department or sub-group level reduce the opportunities for applying the full range of talents in the organization to meeting its challenges.

Development of an organizational vision and mission is a critical transformational leadership function, and those assuming leadership roles feel responsible for helping move the organization forward in the direction of its goals.

In learning organizations, members take responsibility for self-management. The organization may have people in formal managerial positions, but such positions are not considered to prevent the need for such self-management. This contrasts most directly with bureaucratic conceptions of management which are transactional in nature; managers exchange rewards for the services of employees on the assumption that self-interest is the primary motivator of employee action. Leadership in learning organizations is transformational in nature and based on the use of facilitative power. This is a form of power which develops the capacities of others and is in stark contrast to the positional power exercised by more authoritarian leaders in bureaucratic-like organizations (see Dunlap & Goldman, 1991, on this distinction). Transformational leadership is not simply servant-like or democratic, however, as in a communitarian perspective on organizations. Development of an organizational vision and mission is a critical transformational leadership function, and those assuming leadership roles feel responsible for helping move the organization forward in the direction of its goals (Leithwood, 1994).

Learning organizations may have different structures, depending on the particular task to be accomplished and the context in which work is being carried out. Bureaucracies, on the other hand, are predisposed toward exclusively hierarchical structures; communitarian organizations are predisposed toward exclusively flat structures. These structures support very different kinds of decision making as well. In learning organizations, decision making is team-centered. Indeed, it is likely more accurate to consider what teams are doing as more complex than decision making. Structures for decision making in learning organizations are trying to overcome the limitations of what Simon (Newell & Simon, 1972) termed "bounded rationality," and they realize the advantages of many minds working together on the same problem. We characterize this as post-rational because, while it is clearly a systematic process, it extends beyond what is possible with the individual-centered decision making evident in bureaucracies.

Although extensive in bureaucracies, formal policies and procedures are minimized in schools and districts that act as either communities or learning organizations. In learning organizations, however, those policies that do exist are designed not so much to restrict activity as to ensure that the full capacities of the organization's members can be used, without impediment, to move the organization forward. Policy coherence and integration is an important part of this.

Finally, relationships with the outside community also differ considerably depending on which organizational perspective one adopts. Learning organizations are likely to have still quite formal relationships with their outside communities, clearly seeing their role as one of providing service to those communities, but in partnership. Partnership in this case means that they are highly attentive to the expressed needs of the community and highly responsive in attempting to meet those needs. Such responsive partnership, however, still makes it clear that the school and the district are accountable to their local communities for the services they provide, whereas accountability relationships in more communitarian perspectives become blurred.

❇   ❇   ❇   ❇   ❇   ❇

SUMMARY

This chapter unpacked some of the basic assumptions upon which we built the monitoring system. In brief, we assumed that many current restructuring initiatives pursue a defensible image of the educated person of the future; they also identify basic principles for the development of curriculum and instruction that are consistent with contemporary professional and research-based knowledge. Significant progress toward achieving these aspirations, however, will require changing more than the direct curriculum and instructional services provided to students (first-order changes): It will require complementary changes to the basic organization of schools and districts (second-order changes).

Although some second-order changes have been initiated by schools and districts, the basis for selecting such changes usually has been intuitive and/or piecemeal. A coherent perspective on schools and districts as organizations provides the basis for systematically generating a more comprehensive set of second-order changes, perhaps in support of centrally initiated policies and aspirations. Among those alternatives with potential relevance for this purpose, the most promising perspective conceives of schools and districts as learning organizations. This view is most promising because the assumptions it evokes about very basic aspects of human nature as well as about more explicit features of school districts are more defensible. Clearly part of a learning organization perspective, for example, are contemporary assumptions about learning and workplace motivation. Also associated with this perspective, for example, are more defensible assumptions about such features of the organization as its mission and goals, its culture, and the nature of its leadership.

The most serious criticism we can imagine of our decision to adopt a learning organization perspective is not that there are *better perspectives*. It is, rather, that it would be more productive to somehow retain *multiple perspectives*, a position advocated by Bolman and Deal (1991) in their text *Reframing Organizations*. As they argue, each perspective on organizations (and theirs are not the same as ours, with one exception) lends visibility and importance to different facets of the organization; to solve some problems, one perspective may offer more insight than others. This, however, is precisely our reason for recommending a learning organization perspective, because it highlights aspects of schools and districts particularly important in responding to calls for serious school restructuring. In addition, while the Bolman and Deal recommendation has considerable merit for purposes of much managerial problem solving, it would be impossibly cumbersome to follow, in our view, when engaged in organizational redesign. In fact, instituting the multiple frames perspective would make it virtually impossible to develop and implement a systematic monitoring system. Nevertheless, having said that, the organizational design underlying the monitoring system does incorporate significant features associated with each of Bolman and Deal's structural, human resource, political, and symbolic frames. This seems to be an inevitable consequence of a serious effort to describe the demands to which any real-life organization must respond.

Given this justification for our choice of perspective on schools and districts, the next chapter explores more directly what organizational learning actually means. We also begin to identify those conditions which give rise to it, conditions which will need to become part of our model school and district. This chapter is longer than others in the book and, we think, a crucial foundation for the monitoring system. But some readers may wish to delay reading it until they familiarize themselves more fully with the specific features of the monitoring system which are described in Chapters 4 through 9.

Chapter 3

What Is a Learning Organization?

Organizational inquiry can proceed only by concerting [initially] inaccessible information, by clarifying obscure information, and by resolving the inadequacies in organizational theory of action (the mistakes, incongruities, and inconsistencies) which clarification reveals. (Argyris & Schön, 1978, p. 85.)

In the previous chapter we clarified some important assumptions underlying the monitoring system. These were assumptions resulting from adoption of a learning organization perspective on schools and districts (rather than a bureaucracy or community perspective). In this chapter we clarify what organizational learning means and identify some of the conditions which effect such learning

THE MEANING OF ORGANIZATIONAL LEARNING

Fiol and Lyles (1985) suggest that:

organizational learning means the process of improving actions through better knowledge and understanding. (p. 803)

Before this definition offers much of value, three sets of related distinctions need to be grafted onto it. One of these distinctions is between *individual* and *organizational* learning. They are not the same thing. Whereas organizational learning always includes individual learning, considerable amounts of individual learning can take place without any organizational learning; organizational learning is not simply the sum of each member's learning. Unlike individuals, organizations do not have brains. They do, however, have "cognitive systems" that permit perception, understanding, storage, and retrieval of information (more about what these are shortly), sometimes in the face of much mobility among individual organizational members. But such learning is by no means automatic. It often fails to occur. For example, the past decade has witnessed a good deal of effort devoted to recording and assessing effective teaching. Nevertheless, the enormous number of insights acquired through trial and error by experienced teachers over their careers about micro-instructional strategies successful with particular kinds of students are typically unavailable to other members of the school organization; they are erased from organizational memory when the teacher retires or moves on.

A second distinction adding meaning to our basic definition of organizational learning is the difference between the *development of understanding* and *changes in action or behavior* that may result from such understanding. Fiol and Lyles (1985) point out that these processes are not as highly interdependent as one might think. Substantial additions to understanding may result in little or no behavior change. And at least small amounts of behavior change frequently take place without triggering any new understanding. Indeed, these different responses are more or less helpful depending on the organization's environment. This theory would argue, for example, that the kinds of turbulent environments many schools find themselves in, at present, recommend substantial efforts to *understand* but only modest *change in actual behavior*. Excessive behavioral change in a turbulent environment causes the organization to lose its sense of direction and stimulates such complex feedback that it becomes impossible to learn from experience. This may lead to random drift in which little is either learned or accomplished. Some current efforts to restructure schools are a case in point. These efforts sometimes proceed on many fronts at the same time. The restructuring "package" or policy may include a bundle of innovations, few of which are actually "debugged." Implementors are expected to do whatever debugging that is necessary for the innovations to have their desired effects. But it is impossible to learn anything meaningful about cause-and-effect relationships when multiple causes (innovations) are being tried simultaneously! As Levitt and March (1988) argue:

> *Overcoming the worst effects of complexity in experience involves improving the experimental design of natural experience. In particular, it involves making large changes rather than small ones and avoiding multiple simultaneous changes. (p. 335)*

In relation to the prevailing advice on school improvement, such a strategy is decidedly counterintuitive—and exceptionally valuable for that reason.

A third distinction, useful in rounding out our meaning of organizational learning, concerns differences in *levels of learning*. The most inclusive distinction is between lower and higher levels of learning (Fiol & Lyles,

Excessive behavioral change in a turbulent environment causes the organization to lose its sense of direction and stimulates such complex feedback that it becomes impossible to learn from experience.

In schools, the dramatic shift from teacher-directed, whole-class forms of instruction to more student-directed, group-based forms of instruction (e.g., cooperative learning) illustrates the meaning of such high-level organizational learning.

1985). Hedberg (1981) refers to "adjustment" learning, "turnover" learning, and "turnaround" learning; Argyris and Schön (1978) distinguish "single-" from "double-loop" learning. These distinctions acknowledge the steady stream of small, incremental adjustments with which most organizations are occupied, on a continuous basis, to fine-tune their businesses within the context of their accepted world views and attendant assumptions. Such changes signal, at most, modest increases in understanding—low-level or single-loop learning. In contrast, high-level or double-loop learning often results in substantial and irreversible changes in the understanding and behavior of organizational members. These changes signify successful challenges to previously accepted assumptions and the development of a new "world view" for the organization. In schools, the dramatic shift from teacher-directed, whole-class forms of instruction to more student-directed, group-based forms of instruction (e.g., cooperative learning) illustrates the meaning of such high-level learning. This shift challenges previously held assumptions about the nature of knowledge, the role of social interaction in learning, the merits of a competitive ethic in the classroom, and the basis of teachers' authority.

Argyris and Schön (1978) propose yet another level of learning. This is a form of learning that emerges as organizational members, together, reflect on the processes by which they become informed and how these processes might be improved—a form of collective "metacognition."

ORGANIZATIONAL LEARNING PROCESSES

Constructivist views of individual learning (see Leinhardt, 1992, for example) conceptualize it as a process of sense-making in which information from the environment is first perceived then encoded, interpreted, stored, and/or retrieved for application to some problem. While these processes assume mental structures in an individual human brain, organizational learning theory identifies analogues to those structures in the organization. These structures as a whole constitute an organization's cognitive system.

Individuals' perceptions of their environment are guided by their personal needs, goals, aspirations, and values.

Individuals' perceptions of their environment are guided by their personal needs, goals, aspirations, and values. Aspects of the experienced environment that appear relevant to such goals are attended to; those considered irrelevant are not. Such perceptual screening and attention allocation is a function of a hypothetical structure in the mind sometimes referred to as the Executive. The organizational equivalents of the mind's Executive include explicit mission statements, organizational goals, aspects of strategic plans, and formal statements of organizational values, ethics, and beliefs. Stories and those implicit norms, values, beliefs, and assumptions making up the organization's culture may also serve this Executive function. Organizational theorists sometimes refer broadly to a "world view" shared by members to mean approximately the same thing.

Levitt and March's (1988) account of organizational learning centers on organizational routines based primarily on interpretations of past events. These routines, adapted incrementally in response to feedback about how well they accomplish outcomes, include the norms, rules, procedures, conventions, and strategies around which organizations are built. Some of these routines serve, for organizations, the same function served for individuals as short-term memory; that is, to search through the contents of long-term memory for previously stored knowledge capable of helping make sense of perceived information from the environment. Examples of organizational search routines that schools sometimes use include limiting the search to what the staff already knows, expanding the search to include other knowledgeable stakeholders, delegating the search to a committee, and initiating a search for relevant research. These routines access at least partly different organizational memories and may result in the retrieval of information varying widely in quality for its intended purpose.

Organizational theorists identify three strategies for learning, distinguished by the source of the information on which each is based. One strategy is trial-and-error learning (or experimentation)—relying on the experience of oneself or others within the school or district. To be effective, this strategy must untangle the causality of events or difficulties in linking one's actions with observed effects. Failure to do so results in "superstitious" learning—the making of incorrect associations between actions and outcomes. Classroom action research is one approach for more systematically untangling the causality of events. A second strategy is to accept the experiences of others, to actively consider ideas generated from outside the organization (Hedberg, 1981; Senge, 1990). This strategy can help a school or district to avoid being held hostage by its previous experiences and continuing to enact highly learned practices (e.g., perfunctory types of teacher evaluation) long after they have become unproductive for the organization. Staff development experiences based on outsiders' ideas are part of the strategy; so, too, is the external component of some school accreditation processes. Finally, organizations can learn by imitating the behavior of other organizations—a strategy manifesting itself, for example, in direct observation by school staffs of the work of administrators and teachers in schools other than one's own.

Organizations, like individuals, have long-term memories.

Organizations, like individuals, have long-term memories. The contents of an individual's long-term memory are referred to as knowledge structures or schema. Brute facts, ideas, concepts, and theories are stored in declarative form—a statement of beliefs (e.g., my colleagues are enthusiastic about our school improvement activities). The guides to action or skilled performance are stored as steps to take, routines to follow, and the like—a procedural form. Retrieval and use of stored knowledge is heavily dependent on the organization of related pieces of information in knowledge structures and the richness of the associations established among knowledge structures. Documents, files, standard operating procedures, and rule books constitute parts of a school or district's long-term memory. So, too, are culture-related understandings among members concerning "how we do things around here." A school's long-term memory is often heavily dependent on its staff's tacit knowledge, something easily lost in the face of significant staff turnover.

CONDITIONS THAT FOSTER ORGANIZATIONAL LEARNING

The conditions that give rise to organizational learning are described here using Fiol and Lyles' (1985) framework of four contextual factors: culture, strategy, structure, and environment. We describe how each of these contextual factors influences learning based, in part, on evidence from our own most recent research and that of our colleagues (e.g., Leithwood, 2000; Leithwood & Louis, 1998).

District/School Culture and Organizational Learning

An organization's culture is defined by the norms, values, beliefs, and assumptions shared by its members: these are manifested in symbols, artifacts (such as buildings), rituals, ceremonies, overriding ideologies, and established patterns of behavior. Culture can often be used to predict the actions of organizational members, as well as the nature and amount of organizational learning. Three features of typical school cultures seriously challenge the possibilities for organizational learning (we know much less about district cultures).

One feature is a norm of equality, autonomy, and isolation (Fieman-Nemser & Floden, 1986). This norm makes it difficult for teachers, for example, to collaborate on the improvement of instruction or to participate in the mutual definition and solution of broader issues in the school. The virtues of more collaborative cultures, in contrast, by now have been well documented (Little, 1982; Rosenholtz, 1989). They include significant opportunities for teachers to learn from their colleagues as well as the development of a shared sense of purpose and collective responsibility in respect to students. Under conditions of collaboration, there is more likely to develop, as well, a norm of continuous professional growth, stimulated and guided by the sense of a compelling mission (Rosenholtz, 1989). This is well illustrated in a study of five schools implementing the Intermediate Program in British Columbia (Leithwood, Dart, et al., 1992). In these schools, efforts to develop consensus about school goals had strong positive effects on staff motivation and commitment: these efforts also led to an increase in collaborative decision making. Greater cohesiveness among staff resulted from such motivation, commitment and decision making. This, in turn, resulted in stronger, more collaborative teaching cultures. More collaborative cultures reflect the goals of a communitarian perspective on organizations but are easily accommodated within a perspective on districts as learning organizations.

Under conditions of collaboration, there is more likely to develop a norm of continuous professional growth, stimulated and guided by the sense of a compelling mission.

A second problematic feature of typical teacher cultures in schools is the "practicality ethic". This is a strongly held value for consideration of "how to" questions at the expense of either tolerance or energy for "what" or "why" questions. A practicality ethic is predictably a part of the culture of any organization in which its members are faced with the need to solve a steady stream of rapidly emerging problems—as teachers are within the structure of existing classrooms and schools, for example. But the practicality ethic limits both individuals and organizations to low-level (Hedberg, 1981) or single-loop learning (Argyris & Schön, 1978). There is no time and little inclination to visit taken-for-granted assumptions on which school action is based. And yet, in the absence of school staff's thinking deeply about what they are doing and why, the initiative for school "restructuring"—clearly a product of double-loop learning—inevitably will come from outside the school, as it almost always has in the past. Not until school staffs are in a position (financial and otherwise) to propose forms of restructuring meaningful to them will there be a better match, than has often been the case in the past, between reforms proposed for schools and the ecology of teaching and learning.

The third feature within the culture of teaching and the teachers' culture in many schools is a tradition of oral (nonwritten or otherwise recorded) communication. This oral tradition minimizes opportunities for individual and organizational learning in several ways. Teachers' own knowledge about a large proportion of their practices remains tacit and, therefore, largely unavailable to them for their own individual assessment and refinement (this is not a necessary outcome of an oral tradition but seems to be the actual consequence, in the case of teaching). Encouraging journal-keeping, developing video recordings of teaching for subsequent consideration, and writing more formally about what one does are ways to help teachers become more aware of what they do, so that then they can consider the reasons for what they do. As a result of generating such records of their practices, it becomes possible for teachers inside and outside the immediate school context to learn from their colleagues. Such records also provide an organizational memory about the technical core of schooling—the most important and, to date, the least well-stored aspect of what schools do. One school in the Leithwood, Dart, et al. (1992) study provided a dramatic illustration of a principal and staff who understood the importance of recording their experiences for purposes of both their own reflection and the learning of others. The staff wrote a 32-page booklet describing their first-year experiences with the Intermediate Program of the province's policies and directions; what they did, how it worked, what they would change, and the like. This activity was aided by a Ministry grant the first year but continued without such funds in the second year because the staff felt there was so much to be learned from it.

Encouraging journal-keeping, developing video recordings of teaching for subsequent consideration, and writing more formally about what one does are ways to help teachers become more aware of what they do, so that then they can consider the reasons for what they do.

Within a school, providing opportunities for teachers to make such records and to deliberate about them with their colleagues would be an initiative contributing to important aspects of single-loop organizational learning. This responds to what Levitt and March (1988) label *The Redundancy of Experience Problem*:

> ***Ordinary learning tends to lead to stability in routines, to extinguish the experimentation that is required to make a learning process effective.*** *(p. 333)*

People overlearn habitual responses and continue to use them long after they could have been replaced by more effective responses.

Strategies for improvement adapted by a school or a district are a function of the organization's learning capacity, as well as an influence on that capacity. These strategies determine the goals that will be pursued as well as the range of actions for pursuing them. "Thus," as Fiol and Lyles argue, "strategy influences learning by providing a boundary to decision making and a context for the perception and interpretation of the environment" (1985, p. 805). Several of the case schools in the Leithwood, Dart, et al. study (1992), for example, had engaged in prolonged and highly participative processes resulting in clear and widely agreed-upon goals as well as multiyear evolving plans for achieving them. In each case, this "strategy" became the primary lens through which staff interpreted district and provincial initiatives for change. When these initiatives were viewed as meaningful in relation to their school strategy, staff responses to the external policies and directions were positive and opportunistic, in the best sense. But aspects of the external initiatives falling clearly outside the school strategy were largely ignored.

District/School Improvement Strategies and Organizational Learning

A district or school's decision-making structures have a substantial influence on the flexibility of organizational members. More centralized, hierarchical structures are often efficient for reinforcing past behavior and ensuring the reliable performance of routines. Such structures, however, are not well suited to adaptation of organizational practices. Indeed, they too are responsible for *The Redundancy of Experience Problem*, a problem which also arises, as we noted, from the oral communication tradition embedded in the culture of many schools.

Decentralized structures, in contrast, encourage learning and reflective action-taking. They do this by spreading, to multiple members of the organization, the demands for thinking about new information. As Galbraith (1977) explains, this reduces the cognitive workload of individuals, making it easier for them to assimilate those new patterns of practice anticipated, for example, in response to restructuring policies. Senge's (1990) explanation of team learning reinforces Galbraith's claim. All five schools in the Leithwood, Dart, et al. (1992) study demonstrated sensitivity to the need for decentralized structures. This was a natural part of the working style among the seven staff members of Family Elementary School. The four larger schools delegated a considerable amount of leadership. The influence of such delegation on the school improvement process was

District/School Structure and Organizational Learning

always medium or high and positive. Leadership delegation always fostered the development of collaborative decision making which, in turn, always contributed positively to staff development activities—a good proxy for organizational learning since it was directly linked, in all schools, with teachers' professional growth.

These conditions hardly break new ground in our knowledge about structures that foster district and school change. The virtues of shared decision-making structures are supported by a long and venerable body of research (e.g., Conley, 1991). What remains surprising is that so many district and school administrators still believe that such decentralized structures are a challenge to their authority and responsibility. There is considerable practical work to be done in helping such administrators reconceptualize the basis for their authority and develop the skills required to assist their staffs in thinking well collectively. As Senge (1990) claims:

One function of leadership in restructuring schools is to nurture the collective IQ of teams who are working together within the school.

> *Team learning is vital because teams, not individuals, are the fundamental learning unit in modern organizations . . . unless teams can learn, the organization cannot learn. (p. 10)*

So leaders of districts and schools need to develop, with staffs, ways of working together in order to answer this question, also posed by Senge:

> *How can a team of committed [teachers and administrators] with individual IQ's above 120 have a collective IQ of 63? (p. 9)*

District/School Environments and Organizational Learning

A substantial determinant of the extent to which organizational learning takes place is the amount of "turbulence" in both the external and internal environments of the organization. Turbulence, in this case, means complexity and instability. So, for example, districts and schools situated within either local communities or larger regions (the state) which are undergoing significant and rapid political, demographic, and/or economic changes are faced with turbulent external environments. A potentially turbulent internal environment exists when a school is confronted with demands from outside to change rapidly (and perhaps in parallel) its student assessment practices, student grouping practices, relationships with parents, internal governance structures, and other features often associated with restructuring.

Potentially turbulent internal environments can also result from rapid staff turnovers, either administrators or teachers. The general prediction offered by organizational learning theory is that when environments remain too stable, there is little incentive to learn or to change behavior. On the other hand, when environments become too turbulent, organizational members have difficulty understanding what is happening, how they ought to alter their practices in response, and what the consequences are when they do alter their practices. Like Baby Bear's porridge, the amount of turbulence has to be "just right."

Organizational learning that leads to intelligent behavior involves, as Fiol and Lyles assert, "... the creation and manipulation of this tension between constancy and change" (1985, p. 805). They also point out that

> *the level of stress and the degree of uncertainty about past successes determine the effectiveness of the conditions of learning ... and they also influence how the environment is perceived and interpreted. (p. 805)*

When environments become too turbulent, organizational members have difficulty understanding what is happening.

Many North American school districts undoubtedly find themselves in relatively turbulent external environments. Governments change, the economy is in uncertain condition, and the past ten years have witnessed dramatic changes in the demographic makeup of many school communities. Often districts and schools have little or no control over this external environment. However, they can modulate the amount of turbulence experienced in their internal environments. Decisive action to control internal turbulence can take many forms. Implementation timelines that stage the introduction of change is one form used by many districts and schools. Also turbulence-reducing for districts and schools is the systematic development of a mission and / or a set of goals for which there is a high level of consensus among staffs. Such goal clarification narrows staff members' cognitive load to an amount they believe can be meaningfully processed and mastered. Subjectively defining what can be mastered is crucial since there are substantial variations across schools and staffs in their starting points for change and their capaci-ties for changing.

Goal consensus is a powerful influence on the development of teacher commitment.

This mechanism for managing the turbulence of the internal environment contributes to progress in predictable ways. Goal consensus is a powerful influence on the development of teacher commitment. Such commitment is partly a function of motivation which is, in turn, influenced by people's sense of the achievability of the goals they are considering (Bandura, 1986). In districts and schools, goal consensus can contribute to the willingness of staff to engage in more collaborative forms of decision making. As Rosenholtz (1989) explains, shared goals provide a reason for shared decision making about how they can be accomplished and a collective sense of responsibility to those ends.

It is also useful to draw attention to one response to change, widespread among schools historically, which may be termed a "learning disability." This disability, making many small superficial changes, arises from what Levitt and March (1988) claim to be impatience in responding to The Complexity of Experience Problem:

> *Organizational environments involve complicated causal systems, as well as interactions among learning organizations. The various parts of the ecology fit together to produce learning outcomes that are hard to interpret. (p. 333)*

This seems to be an especially important condition to consider in the face of most state restructuring initiatives. These initiatives typically are multidimensional. Many staffs embrace the philosophical foundations upon which these restructuring programs are built. And schools are under significant pressures from their external environments to do something different. These conditions act like steroids for the growth of the "many but small changes" strategy. An important function of leadership under these conditions is to create an appreciation for how a "few but large changes" strategy will be better for the long-term health of a district's schools.

✳   ✳   ✳   ✳   ✳   ✳

SUMMARY   A learning organization is a group of people pursuing common purposes (individual purposes as well) with a collective commitment to regularly weighing the value of those purposes, modifying them when that makes sense, and continuously developing more effective and efficient ways of accomplishing these purposes. After Bereiter and Scardamalia's (1994) conception of "fluid" expertise, this group of people continuously works on the edge of their collective competences. They are engaged in progressively refining their understandings of the problems which populate their organizational context as well as solutions to these problems.

Thinking about schools and districts responding to restructuring initiatives as learning organizations is productive on several counts. First, this perspective acknowledges that many schools and districts will have to make substantial changes in order for the goals of restructuring to be achieved. But the precise nature of many of these changes remains to be discovered. Furthermore, those in the best position to discover many of the needed changes will be local educators, not distant policy makers or researchers. Second, a learning organization perspective focuses primary attention on the processes in which people need to engage in order to figure out what the organizational goals should be and how those goals can be accomplished: Organizational structures are designed as supports for people engaged in such processes. Form follows function rather than the reverse. Finally, conceiving of schools and districts in this way generates quite direct implications for monitoring activities: These activities potentially should provide everyone in the organization with high-quality information useful to them in learning how they can better contribute to accomplishing the school's and/or district's purposes better and to determining what those purposes should be.

PART II: EDUCATIONAL INPUTS AND OUTCOMES

What a school or district begins with—its resources, students, and the like—traditionally have had a critical bearing on what it is able to accomplish on behalf of students and their communities. One likes to think that district and school processes add value to those "inputs." But the school effects research of the 1960s (e.g., Coleman, 1987) garnered so much attention at the time precisely because its results were interpreted as raising serious questions about whether the value added by schools justified their enormous cost.

This interpretation of the school effects research gave rise to the effective schools movement. It was a search for effects, galvanized in large measure by the conviction that schools were about the only viable hope for reversing the fortunes of disadvantaged children. The circumstances in which disadvantaged children found themselves often conspired to undermine the value schools intended to add to the capacities which these children brought to school. So the point of introducing the next two chapters about school district inputs and outcomes together is to make clear that they are closely related. One important goal for a district is to diminish this relationship for children in disadvantaged circumstances by adding value to the Inputs with which the district begins. To do this requires good information, appropriately analyzed about both inputs and outcomes.

Chapter 4

What Are Schools Given to Work With?

OVERVIEW

"Inputs" has a distinctly systems-like (even bureaucratic) ring to it. The term suggests a set of givens with which school districts must contend but over which they have little influence. And while this impression is consistent with the origins of the term, it captures only a portion of our meaning as the term is used in the monitoring system. The broad social and cultural context within which districts function is part of our meaning of inputs; these are referred to as *indirect inputs*. Also included in our meaning of inputs are phenomena which some schools and districts typically consider to be givens but over which they could exercise influence if they chose—*alterable direct inputs*. And finally, included as inputs are phenomena that schools and districts essentially have no chance of influencing—*unalterable direct inputs*. These last two categories of Inputs are referred to as *direct* because their relationships with district and school processes are relatively obvious and predictable whereas *indirect inputs* have more diffuse and much harder to predict relationships.

Only one *indirect input* is included in the ideal school and district:

- **Social climate and culture** (of both the local community and the broader community insofar as it influences students' orientations to education)

Unalterable direct inputs include the following:

- Family background
- Student background

Alterable direct inputs include the following:

- Family's educational culture
- Teacher characteristics and capacity
- Administrator characteristics and capacity
- Facilities, equipment and materials
- Financial resources

That the broader social climate and culture within which schools function ought to be considered as part of the monitoring system can be justified by reference to common experience. For example, rural community cultures of the early 20th century gave priority to the completion of farm work over participation in formal education. This seems likely to have had effects on school attendance and identification comparable to those contemporary urban and suburban cultures that endorse extensive student participation in part-time jobs. As another example, the prolonged, recessionary economic context of the early to mid-1990s is one in which even many highly trained university graduates were unable to find work. On the one hand, this example hardly provided compelling support, in the minds of many students, for the argument that staying in school was critical to their employment opportunities. On the other hand (and somewhat paradoxically), reduced employment opportunities are often the single most powerful explanation for increases in a school's student retention rates. As compared with the street, school looks a whole lot warmer and inviting, never mind that it does not appear to guarantee a job.

The indirect input *social climate and culture* incorporates several elements of what the indicator system developed by the U.S. National Center for Education Statistics (NCES) refers to as the "issue" of Societal Support for Learning—as NCES claims in its report *Education Counts* (1991):

> *An indicator system that ignores the family, communities, and public support (including financial support for schools and colleges) will be seriously flawed.* (p. 26)

Social climate and culture encompass two of the four "concepts" included in the NCES issue Societal Support for Learning: community support and cultural support.

The monitoring system considers only family and student background inputs to be essentially unalterable in the face of actions a school or district itself might initiate. A reasonable question to ask, of course, is, Why include such characteristics or phenomena if there is nothing to be done about them? The answer is found in their power to explain variation in the outcomes achieved by different groups of students. How much variation? We won't hazard a precise estimate. But it is not insignificant. Among

RATIONALE FOR THE MONITORING SYSTEM'S INPUTS

Indirect Inputs

Unalterable Direct Inputs

psychometricians and others with a measurement bent, this means that when achievement is compared across groups of students, schools, districts, or even states and countries, failure to "partial out" or "take into account" differences in family and students' backgrounds is a symptom of gross naïveté. But, like the flu, there is a lot of it going around these days.

Family background characteristics. With respect to family background, at least five characteristics reasonably could have been included in the monitoring system: This would have been warranted, for example, by evidence reported in Scott-Jones's (1984) still relevant extensive review of family influences on cognitive development and student achievement. Several reviews of research on factors influencing student dropout (e.g., Radwanski, 1987; Rumberger, 1983, 1987) also provide such warrant. These characteristics included maternal employment, number of parents, family size and configuration, family income, and family occupational status. Only the last three were selected for the monitoring system, however, because of the superior weight of evidence in support of their influence and our continued determination to design a practical monitoring system.

Aspects of family configuration about which there is significant research include not only family size but also birth order and spacing between siblings.

Aspects of family configuration about which there is significant research include not only family size but also birth order and spacing between siblings (e.g., Scott-Jones, 1984). In much of this research, these variables are considered to contribute jointly to the intellectual climate of the home for the child. That is, (a) family members at a relatively high intellectual level are assumed to provide a better intellectual climate than members at a lower level, and (b) the effects of family members accumulate as the number of members increases. Known as "confluence theory," these assumptions predict intellectual advantages to children lower in the birth order in larger, well-spaced families. However, support for these predictions is quite weak.

Total family income is known to contribute both indirectly and directly to school success. Direct effects are noted by Radwanski (1987), for example, who reports 3% to 10% of Ontario dropouts citing financial difficulties as a central reason for leaving school.

Radwanski found 4% of dropouts in the United States citing this reason. Excessive part-time work (more than about 15 hours per week), sometimes a response to inadequate family income, is also related to dropping out. Family income also influences physical living conditions, leisure activity, and the like which may contribute to school success. However, family income is confounded, as an explanation, by family education level and occupational status; levels of both are associated with dropping out. Scott-Jones (1984) reviews evidence suggesting that gender directs this effect. That is, mothers' educational level has a greater effect on daughters' intellectual development, whereas fathers' educational level has a greater effect on that of sons.

Student background characteristics. A wealth of evidence links student background characteristics to a wide array of student outcomes. For example, all 26 studies included in Glasman and Binianimov's (1981) review of input-output research included attention to student background characteristics. Both gender and preparation for school (e.g., kindergarten, attendance) were among the qualities significantly related to such outcomes as academic achievement and attitudes and, in the case of gender, secondary school completion. To these characteristics, which are included in the monitoring system, we added stability of the educational environment (e.g., student turnover). Inclusion of this characteristic acknowledges the transience of large proportions of the student population especially in some urban schools serving children from economically disadvantaged families (e.g., Linehan, 1992).

When student demographics are framed as an equity issue, the educational goal created for schools and districts is to reduce their power to predict variation in student outcomes.

These student background characteristics encompass significant aspects of NCES's concept of "student demographics," part of the equity issue in its indicator system. When student demographics are framed as an equity issue, the educational goal created for schools and districts is to reduce their power to predict variation in student outcomes. For example, gender has consistently predicted science and math achievement in particular, with males consistently outperforming females (Fraser, Walberg, Welch, & Hattie, 1987). Many recent policy initiatives, as a result, have been aimed at moderating these predictable effects of gender through district and school processes. These student background characteristics are part of other indicator systems, as well.

Alterable Direct Inputs   Among the inputs included in this category, most are routinely considered to be alterable, at least in the long run. This is not the case with family educational culture, however. While schools and districts typically treat these cultures as givens, recent evidence suggests that they can be influenced significantly by school or district initiatives. The growing involvement of formalized parent associations may be a recognition that family educational culture can be changed. Furthermore, the power of such culture to explain variation across schools on such important student outcomes as retention and identification with school is impressive (Leithwood, Cousins, & Gérin-Lajoie, 1993; Leithwood & Jantzi, 1999).

Family educational culture. Family background characteristics contribute directly to the creation of an educational culture in the home—the assumptions, norms, values, and beliefs held by the family about intellectual work, in general, school work in particular, and the conditions which foster both. A substantial body of evidence (e.g., Bloom, 1981; Finn, 1989; Rumberger, 1983, 1987; Scott-Jones, 1984; Walberg, 1984) identifies as many as eight dimensions of either the family's educational culture or resulting behaviors and conditions demonstrably related to school success. Taken as a whole, these dimensions represent what Walberg (1984) refers to as the alterable curriculum of the home. This curriculum, according to his analysis, is *twice as predictive of academic learning as students' socioeconomic status.*

Of the eight possible dimensions of family educational culture (summarized by Leithwood & Joong, 1993), four were included in the monitoring system. These were dimensions about which it seemed feasible to collect information: parental education, family travel, time spent with children engaged in educational activity (e.g., homework), and television viewing.

Family educational culture provides socio-psychological conditions that influence directly the students' motivation and opportunity for intellectual development in school and broader life contexts.

Coleman (1966) refers to effects of these psychological conditions as the "social capital" that students bring with them to school. Such capital is an important determinant of students' capacity to gain access to the knowledge potentially available through the school program (Driscoll & Kerchner, 1999).

Staff characteristics. Two alterable direct inputs included in the monitoring system are characteristics of both teachers and administrators. In each case, education, age and experience, stability, availability, and commitment are considered useful characteristics for description. Specialization is an additional characteristic important to describe for teachers.

These characteristics are intended as estimates of the *potential* that staff possess for providing high-quality service to students although, clearly, they are not even proxies for such service—hence their designation as inputs. Such characteristics, as they apply to teachers, are commonly found in most indicator systems (e.g., NCES, 1991; Sheerens, 1990) no doubt because of the predictive power they have demonstrated in input-output studies (Centra & Potter, 1980; Glasman & Binianimov, 1981). In sum, evidence from these studies suggests that optimum effects on outcomes are achieved with higher levels of teacher education, specialization experience, and job satisfaction (commitment) and lower teaching loads (availability). There are reasons to expect approximately comparable, although smaller effects for administrators, but much less evidence supports such a claim.

Family educational culture provides socio-psychological conditions that influence directly the students' motivation and opportunity for intellectual development in school and broader life contexts.

Resources: Non-financial and financial. Non-financial inputs include most of NCES's (1991) concept of "school resources," for example. For purposes of the monitoring system, organizational size was included as part of this category of input. By far the majority of evidence available about the effects of size argue that "small is beautiful." This is the case at both the district and the school level (e.g., Fowler & Walberg, 1991; Haller, 1992; Monk, 1984). Recent evidence suggests, however, that the location of the district or school (urban vs. suburban vs. rural) mediates the effects of size in different ways (Hanneway & Talbert, 1993). Also, in high schools at least, reduced size has a greater influence on learning in schools with high proportions of minority students and students with lower socioeconomic backgrounds (Lee & Smith, 1997). Weaker but still significant positive relationships are reported between newer, higher quality physical facilities, the ready availability of necessary instructional equipment and material, and a variety of student outcomes (e.g., Rutter et al 1979; Weinstein, 1979).

Reviews of input-outcome research by Glasman and Binianimov (1981) and by Centra and Potter (1980) report consistently positive relationships between financial resources (total expenditures, as well as expenditures on such specific aspects of the district or school as instruction and extracurricular activity) and both student retention rates and academic achievement. But this evidence is by no means uncontroversial. Considerable research has failed to find a strong relationship between the measured resources of schools and student performance (e.g., Hanushek, 1997).

INPUT VARIABLES, INDICATORS, AND MEASURES: A SUMMARY

Based on a review of evidence, examples of which have been touched on in this chapter, the following variables (or characteristics), indicators, and illustrative measures of input were included in the monitoring system:

INPUT VARIABLES AND INDICATORS	ILLUSTRATIVE MEASURES
1. Indirect Inputs *1. 1. Social Climate & Culture*	• Extent to which the community and wider norms and values (reflected in the media, etc.) support the district's mission and goals and contribute to students' participation and engagement in schools
2. Unalterable Direct Inputs *2. 1. Family background*	• Number of children in family • Total family income (relation to provincial average) • Type of job held by parents
2. 2. Student Background	• Male/female • Kindergarten, junior kindergarten attendance • Percentage of student turnover
3. Alterable Direct Inputs *3. 1. Family's Educational Culture*	• Number of years of schooling—diplomas, degrees, special training • Number of family trips per year further than 50 miles from home • Time spent reading per week with child • Time spent helping child with homework; discussing school • Number of hours spent per week watching television

INPUT VARIABLES AND INDICATORS	ILLUSTRATIVE MEASURES
3. 2. Teacher Characteristics	• Degrees, diplomas, professional development • Number of years teaching • Number of years at present school • Teaching assignment vs. speciality • Adult/student ratio in classroom • Job satisfaction
3. 3. Administrative Characteristics	• Degrees, diplomas, P.D. • Number of years as administrator • number of years at present school as administrator • Administrator/teacher ratio in school • Job satisfaction
3. 4. Facilities, Equipment, and Material	• Number of students enrolled • Availability of (list facilities and equipment—yes/no response) • Parallel to above measure (indicate whether or not you use what is available)
3. 5. Financial Resources	• Per-pupil expenditures (adjusted to reflect variations in fixed costs due to special characteristics of district)

✳   ✳   ✳   ✳   ✳   ✳

SUMMARY

The surveys appended to this text do not collect much evidence about the inputs described in this chapter. The reason is that most schools and districts have their own records of many of these inputs already in hand. One exception is family educational culture. The appended survey for measuring Student Participation and Identification with school also requests information from students about their families' educational culture.

Chapter 5

What Ought to Be Accomplished?

Kids across the socioeconomic spectrum are not learning the qualities they'll need in the workplace: patience, perseverance and a positive attitude. (Deutschman, 1992, p. 86)

The aim of education is to enable man to be himself, to "become himself". And the aim of education in relation to employment and economic progress should be not so much to prepare young people and adults for a specific, lifetime vocation, as to "optimize" mobility among the professions and afford a permanent stimulus to the desire to learn and to train oneself. (Faure et al., 1973, p. xxxi)

Knowledge is capable of being its own end. Such is the constitution of the human mind that any kind of knowledge, if it be really such, is its own reward. (Newman, 1961, p. 83)

For the [U.S.] dropouts of the high school class of 1981, potential lifetime earnings lost total $228 billion; the lost tax revenues from these earnings are approximately $68.4 billion. (Orr, 1989, p. 9)

Here at a minimum is what we want [from schools], three general goals that stick close to the narrow endeavor of education. These are goals almost no one would argue with: retention of knowledge; understanding of knowledge; active use of knowledge. (Perkins, 1992, p. 5)

The great changes of our time are imperilling the unity and the future of the species, and man's own identity as well. What is to be feared is not only the painful prospect of grievous inequalities, privations and suffering, but also that we may be heading for a veritable dichotomy within the human race, which risks being split into superior and inferior groups, into masters and slaves, supermen and submen. Among the risks resulting from this situation would be not only those of conflict and other disasters (for present-day means of mass destruction might well fall into the hands of destitute and rebellious groups) but the fundamental risk of dehumanization, affecting privileged and oppressed alike. For the harm done to man's nature would harm all men. (Faure et al., 1973, p. xxi)

Is there an issue more fully explored, over a longer period of time, about which there remains more uncertainty or lack of closure than what should be the purposes of education and our schools? No serious contender comes to mind, and that is probably as it should be. The first of the quotations opening this chapter speak to some basic attitudes and dispositions considered critical for the world of work. (What? Not better spelling?) So does the second quotation. Indeed, the desire to "train oneself" suggests a step back from the more specific question of "In what?", similar to the goals of education proposed in the fifth quotation by David Perkins.

The third and fourth quotations remind us that the ends of education can be viewed from highly individual and non-instrumental to largely social and instrumental perspectives (and everything in between). The final quotation casts a different, but still social and instrumental, perspective on the purposes of education: Those are purposes that thrust education into the forefront of societies wishing to redress long-standing racial, ethnic, and economic injustices.

In the face of such uncertainty about the purposes of education, the monitoring system, nevertheless, had to identify a set of "Outcomes" against which to judge the progress of a school and district in becoming more productive or, as we prefer, more "intelligent" about achieving its mission (it is a learning organization, after all). In spite of their variation, there are some distinctions, both implicit and explicit, in the opening quotations that are useful in framing the treatment of school and district outcomes. One distinction is between immediate and long-term outcomes: another is between individual and social purposes for education. Yet another distinction is between knowledge, on the one hand, and more affective qualities such as attitudes and dispositions, on the other.

In Chapter 1, we alluded to a belief we had related to outcomes, the belief that many restructuring efforts in North America were essentially correct in the purposes espoused for education—at least as far as they go. So these distinctions and beliefs were the starting points for selecting the outcomes to be included in the monitoring system. The remainder of the chapter describes the outcomes in more detail and provides additional reasons for their inclusion.

OVERVIEW

One distinction is between immediate and long-term outcomes; another is between individual and social purposes for education. Yet another distinction is between knowledge, on the one hand, and more affective qualities such as attitudes and dispositions, on the other.

RATIONALE FOR THE MONITORING SYSTEM'S IMMEDIATE OUTCOMES

Knowledge, Skills, and Attitudes

No part of the monitoring system engendered more puzzlement as we developed it than which students' knowledge, skills, and attitudes ought to be included among its immediate outcomes. This is a perplexing problem to solve on three fronts. One was, for want of a better term, philosophical: At issue on this front are fundamental value choices regarding which student outcomes best reflect those images of the educated person central to the mission of the ideal school and district. The second front was a pragmatic one: Given the limited time one reasonably can expect students to spend providing data, which small subset of the vast array of philosophically valued outcomes should be given priority? The third front was technical: Among those outcomes likely to be viewed as most valuable and to which highest priority is assigned by many people are also those outcomes least satisfactorily measured on technical grounds. As Windham explains:

> *Often, the more important and appropriate a concept or variable is, the more difficult it may be to specify, the greater the costs or barriers to operationalization, and the more substantial are the methodological limitations on measurement.* (1987, p. 624)

The philosophical part of this problem was solved through school and district choice, a defensible option primarily because most jurisdictions across North America already have devoted considerable effort to the problem.

School and district choice is also the solution offered by the monitoring system to both the pragmatic and technical parts of the problem. Which subsets of knowledge, skills, and attitudes ought to be selected for measurement depends on the priorities of those particular schools and districts using the monitoring system. Presumably, for example, these priorities are informed by local curriculum policies and strategic directions. This being the case, it would serve no useful purpose for the monitoring system to prescribe its own set of priorities. It would be similarly unproductive for the monitoring system to propose choices from the substantial array of measurement instruments and procedures available to collect data about many of the immediate outcomes.

In sum, the monitoring system includes, as immediate outcomes, the knowledge, skills, and attitudes proposed in local policies and directions.

These are sometimes referred to as essential exit outcomes and lend themselves to more specific formulation within each of the school's curriculum areas. Users of the monitoring system are left with decisions to make about which of these outcomes to include in their own data collection and how best to measure the outcomes which they select.

We assume that most schools and districts will choose to use the outcomes against which they are being held accountable by their state or provincial "masters," and on which their performance is ranked in relation to the performance of other schools.

A second category of immediate outcomes included in the district monitoring system is student participation in and identification with the school as a social unit. There are four reasons why this category of outcome was included. The first reason is especially consistent with the monitoring system's central purpose of providing clues for district and school improvement: Some factors giving rise to students becoming at risk are to be found very early in the child's pre-school and school experiences. Patterns of student participation and identification are sensitive to the consequences of these factors as early as the primary grades. Change in a student's participation and identification is a reliable indicator of problems which should be redressed as early as possible (Lloyd, 1978).

Student Participation and Identification

A second, closely related reason concerns student dropout. For many students, dropping out of school is the final step in a long process of gradual disengagement and reduced participation in the formal curriculum of the school, as well as in the school's co-curriculum and more informal social life. Variation in schools' retention rates are likely to be predicted well from estimates of student participation and identification (Finn, 1989).

For many students, dropping out of school is the final step in a long process of gradual disengagement and reduced participation in the formal curriculum of the school, as well as in the school's co-curriculum and more informal social life.

Third, variation in student participation and identification is a reliable predictor of variation in such typical student outcomes as math and language achievement (Finn & Cox, 1992).

Finally, while one hopes that restructuring initiatives have the power eventually to improve a wide array of intellectual and social outcomes, it seems unlikely that initial efforts to implement those practices will have detectable effects, especially on intellectual outcomes. Changes in student participation and identification might be expected fairly quickly, however. Such evidence would provide either the basis for optimism or an early warning that the desired effects of restructuring may not materialize without additional intervention.

The orientation to understanding and measuring student participation and engagement, within the monitoring system, is based primarily on the work of Jeremy Finn. In his paper *Withdrawing From School* (1989), Finn describes and justifies a model, the participation-identification model, which explains dropping out as a developmental process. Put positively, the model explains continuing engagement in school as a function of participation in school activities, which, along with other influences, results in successful performance. Such performance is esteem building and fosters a bonding or identification with the school.

One central concept in the model is identification with school. The terms "affiliation," "involvement," "attachment," "commitment," and "bonding" encompass the two ideas which, Finn (1989) suggests, constitute a good working definition of identification:

> *First, students who identify with school have an internalized conception of belongingness — that they are discernibly part of the school environ-ment and that school constitutes an important part of their own experience. And, second, these individuals value success in school-relevant goals.* (p. 123)

Such identification and engagement with school, an internal state, has been found to mediate a wide range of achievement and behavioral outcomes among students.

The second concept central to the model is overt behavior—students' actual participation in school activities. Finn's review of research identifies four levels or degrees of such participation and suggests a strong relationship between these levels of participation and the extent of students' identification with school. Level One participation involves acquiescence to the need to attend school, to be prepared, and to respond to teachers' instructions. At Level Two, students take initiative in the classroom, are enthusiastic, may spend extra time on school work, and possibly expand their participation into subject-related clubs, science fairs, and the like.

FIGURE 5.1. The Participation-Identification Model (adapted from Finn, 1989)

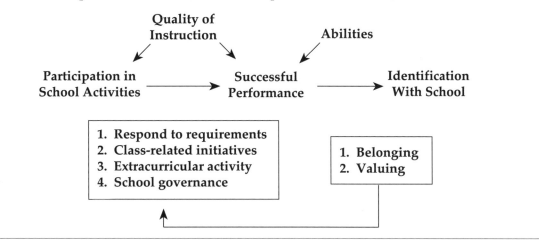

Level Three participation involves participation in school activities outside of the formal curriculum—the social and co-curricular activities of the school, in addition to extensive participation in academic work. Participation in school governance is the Level Four participation in Finn's model.

Figure 5.1 depicts the participation-identification model as encompassing a developmental cycle. Participation in school is essential to successful school performance, although such performance is also influenced by the quality of instruction and student's ability. Quality of instruction is also an influence on participation. Successful performance influences the student's sense of belonging and valuing of school-related goals. Such identification, in turn, has a positive effect on participation.

Participation in school is essential to successful school performance, although such performance is also influenced by the quality of instruction and student's ability.

The survey developed for use in the monitoring system (see Appendix A) to measure participation and identification collects students' opinions about all of the variables shown in Figure 5.1.

Knowledge, skills, and attitudes are immediate outcomes "produced" by a school for (or in) its individual students. But schools are accountable for their contributions not only to individual students but to groups of students, as well. A school's or district's claim that it treats students equally and equitably usually is intended as a claim about its treatment of groups of students distinguished from one another on the basis of, for example, aptitude or ethnicity or location or race—potentially any condition or characteristic that could serve as a criterion for classifying students.

Equality and Equity

Although both outcomes refer to groups of students, however, equality and equity are by no means just different words for the same concept, nor are they either achieved or measured in the same way. Equality has been a goal aggressively pursued by education systems for decades. For example, it was frequently invoked as a rationale for school district consolidation and for the elimination of small schools in the 1960s and 1970s; it has been the basis for many reforms in the provincial funding of education in Canada, for example. In these contexts, equality means ensuring that all groups of students have access to the same level of educational resources. Whether students live in a rural area with a meager tax base, or a wealthy suburban area, equality means making sure that both groups of students have access to the same level of instructional resources, the same types of physical facilities, and the like. Equality means sameness, uniformity, and equivalence.

Equality has been a goal aggressively pursued by education systems for decades.

Equity, a concept which involves standards of fairness and natural justice, is a substantially more complex outcome than equality to achieve or to measure. Whereas equality focuses on a student's access to educational resources, equity focuses on students' access to knowledge (and skills and attitudes). When equality alone is the goal, a school may claim to have achieved it if all students are provided with the same types of educational resources independently of what they learn as a consequence—a focus on the sameness of means. When a school sets itself equity as a goal, it may claim to have achieved it only when all groups of students master the goals of the curriculum to approximately the same degree—a focus in the similarity of ends. Indeed, to achieve equity, a district will most likely have to distribute its educational resources unequally and distribute to different groups of students different types of educational resources. For example, children from homes with impoverished educational cultures may well need the assistance of family support teams (Madden, Slavin, Karweit, Dolan, & Wasik, 1993) in order to overcome a deficit in "social capital" (e.g., education-related attitudes and values) they would otherwise bring to school and on which schools depend so much as a basis for their own work with students (Driscoll & Kerchner, 1999).

Equity, a concept which involves standards of fairness and natural justice, is a substantially more complex outcome than equality to achieve or to measure.

Equality can be estimated by comparing the levels of education resource inputs received by different groups of students: in particular, those inputs described in Chapter 4 as teacher characteristics; administrator characteristics; facilities, equipment, and material; and financial resources. Equity, on the other hand, requires skills and attitudes acquired by groups of students to be compared with those inputs considered relevant in distinguishing among groups of students (e.g., family background, student background): A school or district could legitimately claim to be making progress with its equity goals as such inputs become less and less powerful predictors of groups of students' achieved levels of knowledge, skills, and attitudes.

Most indicator systems measure immediate outcomes. But Windham (1987), among others, has provided a compelling case for the distinction between immediate and long-term outcomes, as well as for including long-term outcomes in an indicator system. These arguments seem to apply equally as well to the monitoring system. In brief, long-term outcomes more closely reflect, than do immediate outcomes, a number of the important reasons causing society to invest so heavily in public education. These reasons concern both the individual welfare of citizens as well as the general public good.

Public investment in primary and secondary education is justified, in substantial measure, by the assumption that it prepares people for life after secondary school. This might be either further education in tertiary education or less formal commitments to continuous learning. Life after secondary school might also mean employment, of course. Two important indications of the contribution a school district makes to individual welfare, then, are students' commitment to further education and/or their preparation for work.

Investments in schools also are justified by their contributions to their local communities. These are aggregate contributions rather than contributions to individuals. And while these contributions depend on outcomes achieved by individual students, they are more and qualitatively different from the sum of these individual outcomes. One of the most obvious indications of outcomes valued within the public good is the contribution the school district makes to a community's economic productivity. Evidence of this indicator can be found in employers' perceptions of graduates as well prepared for entry into their organizations and employers citing the quality of schools as reasons for moving into and/or staying in a community. Real estate agents have become avid users of published school rankings on state achievement tests as a selling tool.

A school or district could legitimately claim to be making progress with its equity goals as such inputs become less and less powerful predictors of groups of students' achieved levels of knowledge, skills, and attitudes.

RATIONALE FOR THE MONITORING SYSTEM'S LONG-TERM OUTCOMES

Individual Welfare

Public Good

People vote with their feet when they select the communities where they will live and raise their children. A central concern in such voting is the quality of the schools in a community . . . [Furthermore,] good public schools, in part, "create" their own political and social communities—by attracting residents who value education and who in turn will support the school's efforts to become even better.
(Crowson, 1992, pp. 97–98)

A second, related, indication of long-term outcomes valued within the public good is the school and district's contribution to a community's quality of life (economic productivity aside). A district may do this, for example, by sharing its physical facilities with the community, by sponsoring non-credit educational programs, by actively participating in community projects, and by its individual members contributing their time and skills to the political life of the community.

OUTCOME VARIABLES, INDICATORS AND MEASURES: A SUMMARY

In this chapter, a brief rationale was offered for the immediate and long-term outcomes included in the district monitoring system except for achievement indicators. Most schools and districts will already have achievement data that can be used in the context of the monitoring system.

VARIABLES AND INDICATORS FOR IMMEDIATE OUTCOMES (OTHER THAN ACHIEVEMENT)

ILLUSTRATIVE MEASURES

---

1. Participation and Identification With School

1.1. Attendance
- Attendance rates

1.2. Participation in school
- Time spent in extracurricular activities
- Willingness of student to complete assigned work
- Degree of active participation in class discussion

1.3. Value associated with schooling
- Students' perception of value of school to them
- Educational and occupational plans of students
- Value of school marks to students

2. Equality

2.1. Similarity of distribution of resources across different groups of students
- Similarity of and access to teacher resources
- Similarity of and access to administrator resources
- Similarity of and access to curriculum materials
- Similarity of and access to physical facilities

3. Equity

3.1. Progress in reducing the contribution of SES, gender, ethnicity, etc. as explanations of variation in achievement and participation and engagement
- Judgments regarding the appropriateness of evidence describing levels of achieved knowledge, skills, and attitudes across different groups of students

VARIABLES AND INDICATORS FOR LONG-TERM OUTCOMES	ILLUSTRATIVE MEASURES

1. Individual Welfare

1.1. *Commitment to further education*
Enrolment in further, formal education

Achievement in further, formal education

- Entrance to postsecondary institutes

- Number of years in postsecondary institutions
- Postsecondary graduation rates

1.2. *Preparation for work*
Engagement in productive employment

- For those not in postsecondary institutions, employed (not at all, part-time, full-time homemaker)

2. Public Good

2.3. *Contribution to community's economic productivity*
Confidence in schools/district by employers

- Extent to which schools are perceived by employers as preparing future employees well
- Extent to which employers cite schools as reason for moving in, staying in, or moving out of community

2.4. *Contribution to community's quality of life*
Sharing of physical facilities

- Proportion of schools making facilities available to community groups

Provision of noncredit educational programs

- Number of noncredit programs available
- Proportion of community participating in such programs

Participation of staff and students in wider life of community

- Numbers of staff and students involved in community projects
- Numbers of staff and students involved in political life of the community

❋ ❋ ❋ ❋ ❋ ❋

SUMMARY

Chapter 10 addresses issues concerning the measurement of immediate and long-term outcomes. As in the case of inputs, we assume that relevant information can easily be obtained by, or is already available to, many schools and districts about most of the long-term outcomes, in particular. With respect to achievement outcomes, we simply recommend using instruments already available. Appendix A, however, does include a survey for measuring student participation and engagement. Our experience with this instrument suggests that most school staffs find the information it generates exceptionally useful in understanding the effects of their work on students.

PART III: CRITICAL PROCESSES AND CONDITIONS

A Systems Orientation to the Core Technology of Schooling

Like many other religions, Christianity depicts the loss of innocence as a fall from grace and blames it on the snake-like embodiment of the devil itself. Of course, many people consider Eden to be about as exciting as watching paint dry: For them, real life couldn't possibly begin until the post-bite period. And one doesn't have to consort with the devil to hold this view—only to value wisdom over innocence, complexity over simplicity, and knowledge over naïveté.

Nevertheless, there is a tone and quality to much professional conversation about what really counts in schools that resembles in its innocence, simplicity, and naiveté, Eden-like images of human nature. "The only things that really matter," according to this view, "are what happens in the classroom." Or, "only the interaction between students and teachers accounts for learning; everything else is largely irrelevant," some claim. "Spending money outside the classroom (while apparently necessary for some unfathomable reason) is to be minimized—cut the administrative fat," so this argument runs. "You're the school district's director of planning! Why don't you get a real job?" We could go on, but you get the idea.

Lest we be accused of implicitly but unfairly picking on one group of professionals over another, the naive view is unconstrained by role boundaries. Those in different roles, however, may be attracted to the view for different reasons: teachers because it places them at the apex of education's status hierarchy; school administrators because it prevents them from having to think seriously about the multidimensional nature of their responsibilities; superintendents because it reduces the need to listen attentively to voices in the community demanding to be heard; researchers because it simplifies the "independent variables" they need to consider in building explanations for school effects; and policymakers because it provides justification for taking money from schools to spend on other priorities.

A naive view of the core technology of schooling, in spite of—indeed, because of— its widespread popularity, is arguably the single best explanation for the historical failure of planned change in schools. Change initiatives typically have concerned themselves with classroom curriculum and instruction and have neglected to consider the interdependence of classroom practices and the organization's structure and culture within which they are enacted (Sarason, 1990). As a consequence, the vast majority of these initiatives have never reached the stage of becoming institutionalized. Some changes have been worn down by these unaltered supports for the status quo until they are indistinguishable from the status quo; "new math" suffered this fate in the 1970s and current reforms in mathematics teaching may be experiencing something very similar (e.g., Ball, 1990). Others, more dramatically, have been surrounded and repulsed in much the same way that white cells deal with foreign organisms in the bloodstream; this was the case with dual entry policies in British Columbia in the early 1990s.

To begin to consider the relationships among classroom practice and school and district structures and cultures would exemplify Senge's (1990) meaning of "systems thinking." According to Senge, this kind of thinking is still rare in most organizations (his "fifth discipline"), not just schools, but it is characteristic of learning organizations. The four chapters in this section describe the product of efforts to exercise the fifth discipline. As mentioned in Chapter 1, the seven dimensions around which these chapters are organized come from a modified version of what Galbraith (1977) identified as aspects or features critical in explaining the effects of any organization. With respect to each of these dimensions, characteristics, conditions, and processes (subsequently they are referred to simply as "processes") are described. These are the processes that seem most capable, in light of current evidence, to add sufficient value to the school and district inputs described in Chapter 4 to accomplish those outcomes described in Chapter 5. The appendixes include surveys for measuring each of the seven sets of processes at both the school level (Appendix A) and the district level (Appendix B).

Chapter 6

Mission and Goals, Organizational Culture

This chapter is concerned with district and school purposes or directions for which there are two sources. The official source of purposes is statements describing the district's or school's mission and goals—the statement of purpose and function of the organization. An implicit source of direction is to be found in the norms, values, beliefs, and assumptions shared by members of the organization—the organization's culture. Depending on the form and content of the culture, these two sources of direction may be mutually supportive, unrelated, or actually in conflict.

An organization's mission and goals may be powerful determinants of organizational learning. This is the case when the mission and goals are used by members of the organization to help them understand and evaluate information coming to them from outside sources, such as the state or department of education, for example, or as feedback from actions taken within the district or school. Serving as "perceptual screens," the mission and goals potentially help people decide what to attend to from the full array of demands, expectations, and information with which they come into contact. When members of School District #98 receive information about how the state fared in the most recent round of national achievement testing, the information itself offers little help in predicting their response. However, if an already established district goal is to improve literacy levels, for example, it is safe to assume that the achievement test results will be seen to be related to that goal.

Use of the organization's mission and goals to interpret information from the environment is an extremely important function, of course, because the broader environments in which schools and districts find themselves are often highly turbulent. Those environments present multiple and conflicting demands—"pay more attention to the basics" *and* "add AIDS education to the curriculum"; "be more accountable to the public" *and* "increase teacher empowerment"; "teach children not subjects" *and* "make sure the expectations of universities for entering students are met." Faced with potentially conflicting demands such as these, the school's or

Organizations vary in the number and complexity of their goals. The goals of McDonald's are fewer, less complex, and less controversial than those of Harvard. That is part of the reason it is so much harder to get agreement on goals among members of an educational or human services organization. To complicate matters further, the stated goals of the organization are not the only, or the most important, goals it pursues. *(Bolman & Deal, 1991)*

DISTRICT AND SCHOOL MISSION AND GOALS

Serving as "perceptual screens," the mission and goals potentially help people decide what to attend to from the full array of demands, expectations, and information with which they come into contact.

district's mission and goals may serve as instruments for deciding which set of demands, if any, deserve attention or where to locate some legitimate middle ground.

But an organization's mission and goals serve as instruments for sense-making and choice only to the extent that individual members of the organization understand them and adopt them as guides to their own personal-professional decisions and actions. Without such understanding and adoption, a mission statement serves, at best, as a public relations tool—as a hollow sop to the public expectation that schools and districts will have a clear sense of direction for which they are accountable.

As a minimum, then, to serve as a stimulus for action, organization members need to be aware of its mission and goals.

As a minimum, then, to serve as a stimulus for action, an organization's members need to be aware of its mission and goals. Furthermore, these mission and goals must be clear and personally meaningful; this is most likely to be the case when the mission and goals are expressions of fundamental values held by organizational members. When these conditions are met, the organization's mission and goals will be used as criteria for decision making at every level. Such active or real use of the mission and goals is more likely when they are seen as dynamic, when they are subject to continuous review and refinement.

The variables, indicators and measures concerned with organization mission and goals, almost identical for districts and schools and included in the monitoring system are as follows:

VARIABLES AND INDICATORS FOR DISTRICT/SCHOOL MISSION AND GOALS	ILLUSTRATIVE MEASURES
1. **Clarity:** *Goals and mission are clear and can be readily understood.*	• Staff express their belief that they understand school goals and mission.
2. **Meaningfulness:** *Goals and mission are considered valuable and worth striving for (commitment).*	• Staff express high levels of commitment to striving for goals and mission. • Goals form a shared ideology to provide a web of identification and affiliation. This inspires loyalty to the district or school.
3. **Awareness:** *District/school staff are aware of goals and mission (consensus).*	• Staff are able to tell what the mission and goals are. • Staff are in agreement about what the school goals and mission are. • Goal statements are in writing.

Variables and Indicators for District/School Mission and Goals	Illustrative Measures
4. **Usefulness:** *Goals and mission influence decisions at district, school, and classroom levels.*	• Goals used as the basis for communicating with others.
5. **Currency:** *Goals and mission are reviewed and revised periodically.*	• Regular evaluation of progress toward mission and goals lead to refinement of goals.
6. **Congruence:** *Goals and mission of school and district are congruent with one another.*	• Staff perceive strong congruence among mission and goals at district and school levels (possibly at state/provincial levels, as well).
7. **Value base:** *Goals and mission are expressions of a set of fundamental values.*	• Perception of staff that mission and goals are direct reflection of a set of basic values. • Staff understand what values are reflected in mission and goals. • Values on which mission and goals are based are a good reflection of individual staff values.
At the school level, in addition:	
8. **Immediate focus:** *Instrumental in fostering productive change.*	• Immediate focus is on teachers' behaviors and the school organization.
9. **Long-range focus:** *Oriented to defensible outcomes for students.*	• Academic focus includes attention to both basic skills and higher order capacities (Intellectual, Social/Emotional, Artistic/Aesthetic, Physical).

The current business literature as well as much writing in education, especially writing about schools, is heavily loaded with talk about organizational culture. Such talk demonstrates the widespread appeal of what Bolman and Deal (1991) call the "symbolic frame" for understanding organizations, as opposed to earlier preoccupations with a "structural frame" (organizations viewed as bureaucracies, for example). Most of this talk, however, is quite loose. For example, empirical evidence about productive school district cultures is limited to only a handful of studies (e.g., Coleman & LaRocque, 1991). This is also the case with evidence about productive school cultures (e.g., Hargreaves & Macmillan, 1991; Little, 1982) and how leaders might change district or school cultures (e.g., Deal & Peterson, 1990; Leithwood & Jantzi, 1990; Musella & Davis, 1991). Furthermore, a synthesis of what we actually know from these studies clearly does not do justice to the complexity of the concept of an ideal organizational culture.

DISTRICT AND SCHOOL CULTURE

We encounter organizational cultures all the time. When they are not our own, their most visible and unusual qualities seem striking. . . . When the cultures are our own, they often go unnoticed—until we try to implement a new strategy or program which is incompatible with their central norms and values. Then we observe, firsthand, the power of culture. *(Kotter & Heskett, 1992, p. 3)*

School and district cultures vary along three dimensions. They may be more or less *strong*, depending on the extent to which staff share taken-for-granted norms, values, beliefs, and assumptions. The specific *nature* of those norms, values, beliefs and assumptions defines the *content* of the culture. Finally, the *form* of an organization's culture may vary from one that largely supports isolated, individual work, and problem solving to one that is based on collaboration in its various forms: collaboration among subgroups in the organization ("balkanized") to whole-staff collaboration.

This section includes some additional conceptual distinctions we consider necessary to more adequately acknowledge the complexity of organizational culture as applied to districts and schools. Incorporated into this summary is available research evidence, supplemented with both professional judgments (those of school and district staff from several of the school districts centrally involved in developing the monitoring system) and most of our conceptual distinctions. While these variables, indicators and measures reflect current thinking about organizational culture reasonably well, they ought to be considered more tentative than such information about many other aspects of the monitoring system.

The power of an organization's culture, referred to in the quotation opening this section, is manifest in at least three distinct areas of an organization's functioning: the manner in which the organization conducts its day-to-day business; its response to specific proposals for change; and its influence, more generally, on the nature and type of organizational learning that occurs. What has yet to be recognized adequately is the flexibility required of a school or district culture to be productive in relation to all three of these functions. Figure 6.1 illustrates what such flexibility means.

Consider, to begin with, the function of conducting day-to-day business in a school. This is a hectic, fast-paced enterprise for both teachers and administrators, not an enterprise that offers much time for individual, never mind collegial, deliberation. To function productively under these circumstances, staff typically must act individually, often in isolation from other staff or, at best, with small groups of immediate colleagues (a balkanized culture). But such individual action must be guided by a set of taken-for-granted norms, beliefs, values, and assumptions about "how we do things around here" for which there are high levels of consensus among most members of staff. Schools become more or less chaotic when such

FIGURE 6.1. A Description of Ideal Organizational Cultures in Relation to Three Areas of District and School Functioning

Objects of Influence by Culture	Elements of Organizational Culture		
	Ideal Strength	**Ideal Form**	**Ideal Content (examples)**
1. Conduct of day-to-day business	• High consensus	• Isolated • Balkanized	**Norms:** *mutual respect among staff* **Beliefs:** *in the dignity and worth of all individuals* **Values:** *participation in decision making by all legitimate stakeholders* **Assumptions:** *all decisions ultimately must be justified in terms of student welfare*
2. Response to specific change initiatives	• Modernate consensus	• Isolated • Balkanized • Collaborative	**Norms:** *openness to change* **Beliefs:** *implementing change involves considerable "local" problem solving* **Values:** *consequences for students/clients* **Assumptions:** *schools/districts are "systems": changing one part has implications for other parts*
3. Organizational learning	• Low to moderate consensus	• Isolated • Balkanized • Collaborative • Cosmopolitan	**Norms:** *risk-taking; use of different perspectives for problem solving* **Beliefs:** *one learns from failure; good ideas may be found in many different places* **Values:** *knowledge, personal mastery* **Assumptions:** *error and uncertainty is inevitable; learning is never-ending*

consensus weakens. As well, empirical evidence does associate the productive conduct of day-to-day school business with particular cultural content, illustrations of which are provided in the far right column of Figure 6.1.

As a second function, districts and schools are required to respond to specific change initiatives, sometimes from within but often from outside—state policies and directions, for example. Productive responses to such change make importantly different demands on the organization's culture than does the conduct of daily business. For example, very strong (high consensus) cultures can be self-sealing, cutting off the inclination to award ideas for change the attention they may deserve. Moderately strong cultures offer more chances for such consideration: Some discussion acts as a stimulant for serious attention to alternative practices and helps avoid the co-optation of these alternatives. Since initiatives for change can arise internally from individuals or small groups, support for both isolated and

When organization-level problem solving is needed to respond to a change initiative, high levels of collaboration may be productive.

balkanized forms of culture will sometimes help stimulate such initiatives. When organization-level problem solving is needed to respond to a change initiative, high levels of collaboration may be productive. Further, whatever *form* of culture is productive in response to change initiatives, evidence suggests that the content of school and district cultures that include norms of openness to change and belief in the need for local adaptation of useful external initiatives are productive. Also productive are cultures that weigh the value of proposed changes primarily in terms of consequences for students and that appreciate the interconnectedness of the elements of the organization.

As we have claimed in previous chapters, a third function of ideal schools and districts is organizational learning. This function, like the previous two, makes its own demands on the organization's culture if it is to be performed well. For example, the high consensus cultures so important for conducting day-to-day business may shut off organizational learning. Indeed, Hedberg (1981) goes so far as to claim that

> *a learning organization should rely on minimal amounts of consensus, contentment, affluence, faith, consistency and rationality . . . for each of these organizational assets, there should be a counterbalancing one.* (p. 22)

As in responding to change initiatives, organization learning demands openness to ideas but from even more diverse sources. For this reason, we have borrowed the term "cosmopolitan" to signify a form of culture which encourages collaboration with ideas and people wherever they may be found (the typical meaning of a "collaborative culture" is one that encourages members within the organization to work together).

The organizational cultures of districts and schools have much in common.

Organizational learning also requires cultural content different from the content which supports other functions: for example, norms of risk taking and experimentation; beliefs about the importance of learning from small failures (or what Sitkin, 1992, refers to as strategic failure). Valuing the continuous development of personal mastery (Senge, 1990) or expertise (not just competence) in one's job is also part of the content of a culture that fosters organizational learning.

The organizational cultures of districts and schools have much in common. Variables, indicators and measures of these areas of similarity and several

of the most important aspects of uniqueness included in the monitoring
system are presented below:

VARIABLES AND INDICATORS FOR DISTRICT AND SCHOOL CULTURE	ILLUSTRATIVE MEASURES

1. Strength of Culture

There is substantial agreement among staff about the bases upon which day-to-day decisions are made.

- When asked, most staff members describe the same bases on which day-to-day decisions are made.

There is moderate agreement among staff about the need for change and the nature of responses appropriate to specific change initiatives.

- Most proposals for change are given serious consideration by staff. Efforts are made to identify the differences as well as the similarities of the change as compared with current practice.

Staff members demonstrate a wide variety of approaches to learning as divergent perspectives on organizational problems and how to solve them.

- In the context of staff meetings, issues are explored from many points of view and individuals do not hesitate to disagree with one another concerning ideas and positions.

2. Form of Culture

Varies by function:

Day-to-day decision making

- Encouragement is provided for individual and small team problem solving.

Response to specific change

- Encouragement is provided for individual, small team and whole school problem solving, depending on the nature of the change.

Organizational learning

- Encouragement is given for all types of problem solving and the consideration of useful ideas, whatever their source.

3. Content of Culture: District and School

3.1. Norms

Mutual respect

- Mutual respect is shown among staff.
- Respect is shown by staff for students and parents.
- All people are to be awarded dignity and respect.

Openness to change

- Continuous professional growth is fostered for all staff.
- Reciprocal influence exists among staff at different levels in the organization.

Risktaking

- Staff demonstrate willingness to try new practices.
- Failures resulting from serious attempts to implement new practices are supported and efforts made to learn from them.

High expectations

- Staff hold high expectations for their own performance.
- Staff hold high expectations for performance of students.

Variables and Indicators for District and School Culture	Illustrative Measures
3.2. Beliefs	
Human potential	• All individuals have the capacity to learn and learning is a personal, life-long experience. • All individuals can experience joy and satisfaction by striving to reach their potential. • Individuals have the power to positively influence their own futures. • Individuals are responsible and accountable for their decisions and actions.
Students	• High self-esteem is essential. • Students are the center of the education system. • Students' opinions are to be sought out and carefully considered in designing their education. • Students should have equitable access to learning opportunities.
Parents and community	• Parents and the community are partners with the school in the education of students.
Working environments	• Safe, healthy, and attractive environments enhance working and learning.
3.3. Values	
A core set of values ought to be reflected in the outcomes of most decision making.	• Virtually all decisions contribute directly or indirectly to student growth and welfare.
A core set of values ought to consistently guide decision-making processes.	• Staff decision-making processes ensure that as much knowledge as possible relevant to the decision is acquired and considered. • Staff decision-making processes encourage those involved to act in accordance with their role responsibilities, when those are clear and with a broad concern for the welfare of the organization and its clients when role responsibilities are unclear.
Assumptions Districts and schools are accountable to their communities and must have the support of their communities.	• Staff members routinely include community members in district and school decisions related to their interests.

4. Content of Culture: School

4.1. Norms

Positive	• Staff express optimism about their impact and enthusiasm for their work.

VARIABLES AND INDICATORS FOR DISTRICT AND SCHOOL CULTURE	ILLUSTRATIVE MEASURES
4.2. Beliefs	
Student-centered	• Staff encourage student self-control and serious attitudes toward school. • Staff are willing to meet with students informally outside school hours. • Staff show empathy and rapport with students. • Staff are sensitive to the age of students and the peer pressures and social interests associated with that age. • Staff hold high expectations for individual student learning and behavior. • Staff provide models of the educated citizen. • There is school-wide recognition of student success. • Teachers are recognized for their exemplary classroom practices (as well as other school-wide or district practices). • Students are recognized for self-directed learning initiatives. • Staff actively model the school's images of an educated citizen. • Staff provide structures for student participation in school governance.
4.3. Values	
Designed to foster student learning	• Planning for and carrying out teaching is regarded by staff as teachers' most important work. • Administrative protection of classroom instructional time is provided. • Teachers are prepared for class, punctual, do not waste time in class, and rarely end class early.
Designed to provide a professional work environment or staff	• Administrative support is provided for professional risk-taking and experimentation. • Staff believe that the school is a "learning system." • Staff show an ongoing interest in their own professional development (e.g., course taking, action research, etc.). • Staff demonstrates high levels of dedication to teaching.
4.4. Assumptions	
Positive	• Minimal emphasis is placed on student punishment and control. • Staff praise and reward students' exemplary industry and behavior.
Safe and orderly	• Staff and students feel physically and psychologically safe in the school. • School is largely free of vandalism and discipline problems. • School carefully monitors student behavior and acts to eliminate inappropriate behavior when it occurs.

✳   ✳   ✳   ✳   ✳   ✳

SUMMARY   Appendixes A and B include four survey instruments for measuring the processes described in this chapter. For mission and goals, there are both district and school surveys. This is also the case for organizational culture.

Chapter 7

The Core Tasks of Planning, Managing, Leading, and Instructing

Four categories of organizational processes are des cribed in this chapter: planning, managing, leading, and instructing. As with other ideal characteristics, conditions, and processes captured by the monitoring system, districts and schools have much in common. But there are aspects of these processes clearly unique to either the district or the school. The text of this chapter will emphasize largely what is common, leaving to the summaries of variables and indicators at the end of the chapter a description of what our review suggests is unique or different about districts as compared with schools.

An organization's mission and goals, as we described in Chapter 6, offers one perspective on its purposes: Its culture embodies a less "official" view of those purposes, as well as some of the basic premises on which are based the actual processes used by the organization in striving to accomplish its purposes. Planning processes are the explicit means for deciding on mission and goals as well as actions to be taken for their accomplishment. As Daft (1989) explains:

> *Under conditions of environmental uncertainty, planning and forecasting are necessary. Planning can soften the adverse impact of external shifting.... In an unpredictable environment, planners scan environmental elements and analyze potential moves and countermoves by other organizations.... As time passes, plans are updated through replanning. (p. 62)*

Plans, however, serve these functions of internal integration and external adaptation only if they actually influence what members of the organization do. And whether or not this is the case depends, in substantial measure, on the nature of planning processes. Evidence suggests that productive planning processes, defined in these terms, are inclusive of those groups touched by the plan. Such processes are evolving, dynamic, and also take account of information provided by those on the delivery end of the school's and district's services. Planning processes with these characteristics lead to the personal internalization, by organizational members, of the resulting plan. When this occurs, a plan is the same as a shared vision of what the organization wants to do. And such vision, as Senge argues,

DISTRICT AND SCHOOL PLANNING

is vital for the learning organization because it provides the focus and energy for learning. While adaptive learning is possible without vision, generative learning [i.e., expanding your ability to create] occurs only when people are striving to accomplish something that matters deeply to them. (1990, p. 206)

Although often considered exclusively a management tool, we have chosen to treat planning separately because of its potential role in the creation of organizational vision. When this potential is realized, planning is as much a leadership function as it is a management function. For this potential to be realized, however, we must move from a transactional to a transformational understanding of planning. From a transactional perspective, planning is, at best, "a goal-setting, sequential, systematic, value-free and quantitatively based activity" (Hamilton, 1991, p. 21) designed to bring rational order and predictability to an otherwise uncertain set of events; at worst it is simply "a ceremony that an organization must conduct periodically to maintain its legitimacy" (Bolman & Deal, 1991, p. 177).

The planning process itself should "aim to inspire and encourage interest and involvement."

In contrast, transformational perspectives on planning are grounded in the appreciation that

the implementation of educational plans depends, in the last analysis, on the will, motivation, identification, and even the internalization processes of teachers, students, parents and administrators participating in the educational process. (Inbar, 1993, p. 174)

Given this appreciation, broad participation of these same people in the planning process is essential. As Inbar also points out, such participation is the means through which the plan is transformed into a symbol of change, and remote ideals and goals take on a concrete reality in the minds of those involved. The planning process itself should "aim to inspire and encourage interest and involvement" (p. 176).

The monitoring system distinguishes between "strategic planning," which districts ought to do in providing a framework for school decision making, and "school planning"—a process for bringing local needs and district goals together into a shared school vision. The following variables, indicators and measures related to district planning are included in the monitoring system.

VARIABLES AND INDICATORS FOR DISTRICT STRATEGIC PLANNING	ILLUSTRATIVE MEASURES
1. Captures relevant information possessed by all appropriate stakeholders; much of this information is provided by the school improvement planning process	• Representatives of all stakeholder groups agree that they have suitable opportunities to inform the strategic plan.
2. Includes a systematic review of the district's current status and identifies areas in which district is or is not meeting current needs of stakeholders, especially with respect to student outcomes	• There is evidence of data having been collected and reviewed about district operations; also, there is evidence of "gap analyses" having occurred.
3. Includes systematic analyses of social, political, economic, and other trends likely to have consequences for districts/schools in the future; they are not only local but also provincial, national, and global trends	• There is evidence of consideration of future "scenarios" based on analysis of relevant trends.
4. Includes as sources of district goals, school goals, parental aspirations, provincial priorities, and political realities	• There is evidence of consideration, in establishing district goals, of a wide array of sources.
5. Encourages collaboration and helps generate high levels of understanding and support, among all stakeholder groups, for the planning process and its outcomes	• All stakeholder groups report understanding of and agreement with the process and its outcomes.
6. Results in a set of district goals sufficiently clear, compelling, and focused so that schools are able and motivated to use them as primary sources of direction in their school-based development	• School development plans explicitly reference the goals of the strategic plan as an important source of direction. • School staffs report having sustained discussion of district goals.
7. Progress in achieving strategic planning goals is monitored regularly and systematically; monitoring results are used as a significant stimulus for organizational learning	• A monitoring process is developed and portions of it implemented annually. • All stakeholders report significant learning as a result of considering the results of the monitoring process. • Incremental improvement in measures of student outcomes are among the criteria used for judging progress.
8. Includes a process for evaluating the strategic planning process to determine its value in achieving the district's mission	• There is evidence that the strategic planning process is evaluated.
9. Results in a bank of data about school district functioning to be used for multiple purposes	• Data bank can be identified.
10. Strategic planning processes and outcomes communicated to all stakeholders regularly	• Stakeholders report receiving regular communication about district planning.

With respect to school planning, the monitoring system includes the following:

VARIABLES AND INDICATORS FOR SCHOOL PLANNING	**ILLUSTRATIVE MEASURES**
1. Captures relevant information possessed by all appropriate stakeholders	• Representatives of all stakeholder groups agree that they have suitable opportunities to inform the school plan.
2. Includes a systematic review of the school's current status and identifies areas in which school is and is not meeting current needs of stakeholders, especially with respect to student outcomes	• There is evidence of data having been collected and reviewed about school operations; also, there is evidence of "gap analyses" having occurred.
3. Includes, as sources of school goals, district goals, parental aspirations, provincial realities, and political realities	• There is evidence of consideration, in establishing school goals, of a wide array of sources.
4. Encourages collaboration and helps generate high levels of understanding and support, among all stakeholder groups, for the planning process and its outcomes	• All stakeholder groups report understanding of and agreement with process and its outcomes.
5. Results in a set of school goals sufficiently clear, compelling, and focused so that staff are able and motivated to use them as primary sources of direction in their work (see School Mission and Goals [1])	• Individual staff explicitly reference school goals as an important source of direction. • School staffs report having sustained discussion of school goals.
6. Progress in achieving school goals monitored regularly and systematically; monitoring results are used as a significant stimulus for organizational learning	• A monitoring process is developed and portions of it implemented annually. • All stakeholders report significant learning as a result of considering the results of the monitoring process. • Incremental improvement in measures of student outcomes is the main criterion for judging progress.
7. Includes a process for evaluating the school planning process to determine its value in achieving the school's goals	• There is evidence of a process for evaluating the school planning process.
8. School planning processes and outcomes are communicated to all stakeholders regularly	• Stakeholders report receiving regular communication about school planning.

Classical management theory includes among those strategies available to managers not only planning but also organizing, supervising, coordinating, and budgeting (e.g., March & Simon, 1958; Massie, 1965); staffing is also an important management function or strategy. The monitoring system describes district-level management more or less in these terms. At the school level, the monitoring system uses modifications of these classical strategies which reflect an emphasis on instructional management, in particular.

Although the monitoring system distinguishes management from leadership, it assumes that both are required for productive schools and districts. The right things need to be done *and* they need to be done right. Indeed, we subscribe to the view that leadership is most frequently exercised *through* the performance of managerial activities. For example, most principals tour the halls of their schools several times a day. This is sometimes referred to as "being visible" and can serve important managerial functions—providing information about the state of the building, discouraging misbehavior in the halls, getting to know the students, and the like. In addition, however, "being visible" can serve leadership functions as well, depending on just what one does while being visible. For example, one can reinforce important cultural norms and values through the form of one's communication with students; one can provide support to individual staff members when the need for such support is evident (e.g., advice on how to manage disruptive student behavior); one can communicate the school's mission by referring to it in one's interactions with students and staff; and one can model the school's image of an educated person. Management and leadership, from this perspective, are distinguishable but interdependent (Duignan, 1988; Hunt, 1991).

Variables, indicators and measures of district-level management included in the monitoring system make two assumptions about district organization. First, district management is assumed to be exercised through departments or teams, each with special but overlapping responsibilities. Second, district management is assumed to be operating within the framework of a district strategic plan; teams normally develop operational plans to determine how they will contribute to the broader goals of the district specified in its strategic plan.

DISTRICT AND SCHOOL MANAGEMENT

Although the monitoring system distinguishes management from leadership, it assumes that both are required for productive schools and districts.

VARIABLES AND INDICATORS FOR DISTRICT MANAGEMENT	ILLUSTRATIVE MEASURES

1. **Operational Planning**: Each team regularly develops, reviews, and refines a plan for its operation. This plan anticipates how the team contributes to
    (a) achieving the district strategic plan;
    (b) district maintenance; and
    (c) services to schools.
Goals, strategies, timelines, responsibilities, and costs are specified by the plan.
	• Analysis of available plans

2. **Information for Planning**: The views of those served by district management teams are collected and considered in the development of operational plans.	• All groups served by district administrative teams know that they have had opportunities to express their views about operational plans. • All groups served by district administrative teams know their views have been given due consideration.
3. **Organizing**: Based on each team's operational plan, as well as the capacities and interests of staff, teams define roles and responsibilities and develop structures to assist staff in carrying out their tasks.	• Team staffs support high levels of coherence between their jobs and the way their units are organized.
4. **Staffing**: Staffing practices help ensure high levels of capacity for contributing to the teams' operational plans and the district's strategic plan. Such practices also encourage commitment to the vision espoused by the district and the team.	• Analysis of criteria used in hiring and objectives on which staff development activities based • Staff express high levels of commitment to the vision espoused by the district and the team.
5. **Supervision and Evaluating**: Performance of staff is monitored in a manner appropriate to the level of responsibility of the position. The goals of the team and the district's strategic plan, as well as the responsibilities outlined in the operational plan, serve as criteria on which supervision and evaluation are based. Staff development and accountability purposes are served by this supervision and evaluation.	• Analysis of criteria used for performance review • There is evidence of the results of performance review leading to the development of staff development planning. • Personnel evaluation processes reference district and department goals.
6. **Coordinating**: Operational plans are coordinated across all teams so that the collective impact of their implementation substantially furthers progress with the district's strategic plan.	• Staff express high levels of consistency across teams/units in their contribution to the district's strategic plan.
7. **Communication and Reporting**: Information about the nature of operational plans and the implementation of team operational plans and the district's strategic plan is disseminated widely across and within teams.	• Members of each team/unit have detailed understandings of the work of other teams/units and how their work is to be integrated as a collective contribution to the district's strategic plan.
8. **Budgeting**: Financial resources are allocated according to priorities identified in the teams' operational plans and the district's strategic plan.	• Members of each team/unit are satisfied that financial allocations are consistent with priorities identified by the district and their team/unit.

The more instructionally-specific management practices, at the school level, included in the monitoring system are as follows:

VARIABLES AND INDICATORS FOR SCHOOL MANAGEMENT	ILLUSTRATIVE MEASURES
1. Staffing is carried out to ensure high quality instruction.	• Principal/staff recruit new staff. • Selection of new staff is guided by systematic process and defensible criteria. • Acculturation of new staff is carried out deliberately, comprehensively, and by many members of staff.
2. Instructional organization fosters continuous instructional improvement.	• Protects instructional time • Coordinates instructional program • Participates in discussions of instructional issues • Secures program resources • Regularly observes classrooms • After observation, helps staff improve effectiveness • Secures resources and technical assistance for staff who need it
3. Monitoring of school activities takes place frequently and regularly.	• Moves constantly through school observing and offering assistance • Is available, accessible, and highly visible • Reviews student progress regularly and takes appropriate action
4. Decision-making processes are well informed and suited to the circumstances.	• Decisions based on good information (from monitoring) • Selects form of decision making to suit task and setting
5. Relations with non-school staff are productive.	• Accessible to parents, often maintaining an open-door policy • Establishes productive working relationships with the community • Secures high degrees of autonomy for the school within the district • Establishes processes and procedures for communicating with non-school staff about school issues (e.g., parent advisory council)

SCHOOL AND DISTRICT LEADERSHIP

Duke's assertion (see side quote) discourages us from defining, in general, the behaviors of effective leaders. Rather, it encourages the view that leadership is situational and context dependent. When staff members experience lack of leadership, the problem may be one of fit. For example, Susan brings to her new job as principal of Overwhelmed Elementary School boundless energy, ambitious visions, and a strong commitment to school reform. But Susan succeeds Tony, who had the same qualities and was successful in helping staff initiate a large bundle of changes in the school during the three years of his tenure. The staff are in the midst of refining their knowledge, "working out the kinks" in these changes, and recovering from the ubiquitous "implementation dip" (Fullan, 1991). The support they need, at this point, is "close to the elbow" technical assistance, a stable school environment with limited distractions from their efforts to

The cognitive perception that leadership exists may be regarded as recognition that a carefully framed situation exists in which actions of a leader, the actions of his followers, and the traditions of their culture are mutually reinforcing and correspondingly meaningful.
(Duke, 1986, p. 18)

consolidate the changes they have made. They also need help in assessing whether the changes they have made are paying off as anticipated. From Susan's perspective, this is somewhat dull work that does not take advantage of her strengths.

As a minimum, then, the orientation of the monitoring system to district and school leadership must acknowledge the importance of situation and context; this means that it must allow for variation in leadership style and behavior. It is possible to do this, however, and still endorse a particular model of leadership when the model fits the broad challenges being experienced by restructuring districts and schools and when considerable variation in behavior within the model is possible. A transformational model of leadership appears to meet these requirements. At the school level, a growing body of evidence suggests that transformational leadership fosters school restructuring (Leithwood, Jantzi, & Steinbach, 1999). Coleman and LaRocque (1991) and Roberts (1985) provide impressive support for this orientation to district leadership, as well.

Roberts' (1985) synopsis of transformational leadership sounds a lot like what Susan is keen to offer Overwhelmed Elementary School:

> *This type of leadership offers a vision of what could be and gives a sense of purpose and meaning to those who would share that vision. It builds commitment, enthusiasm, and excitement. It creates a hope in the future and a belief that the world is knowable, understandable, and manageable. The collective action that transforming leadership generates empowers those who participate in the process. There is hope, there is optimism, there is energy. In essence, transforming leadership is a leadership that facilitates the redefinition of a people's mission and vision, a renewal of their commitment, and the restructuring of their systems for goal accomplishment.* (p. 1024)

But research concerning the meaning of transformational leadership in practice suggests that it is multidimensional (e.g., Podsakoff et al., 1990). It is concerned, as is Susan, with developing a vision, fostering acceptance of group goals, and providing intellectual stimulation. But it is also concerned with providing support to individual staff members as they grapple with changing their practices; it is about displaying high performance expectations in the face of learning new behaviors; and it also includes setting an example for staff to follow that is consistent with the values espoused by the district or school.

Each dimension of transformational leadership can be carried out through a variety of behaviors. Some, like modeling, can be performed through one's everyday managerial activities. As well, some dimensions of transformational leadership will be more suitable to focus on than others in a given context and situation, as Overwhelmed Elementary School reminds us. So like Tony, Susan may offer her school transformational leadership. But unlike Tony, she ought to focus less, for a while, on vision and goals and more on individual support and modeling.

Learning organizations (and perhaps Overwhelmed Elementary School can be one) require transformational leadership because, through its several dimensions, it empowers staff to strive for personal and collective mastery. Such leadership distributes power widely throughout the organization rather than hoarding it at the top. This unleashes staff members' capacities for performance and for further learning.

The variables, indicators and measures of such transformational school and district leadership included in the monitoring system are shown below:

VARIABLES AND INDICATORS FOR DISTRICT AND SCHOOL LEADERSHIP	ILLUSTRATIVE MEASURES
1. Provides vision and/or inspiration	• Has the capacity and judgement to overcome most obstacles • "Excites" staff with vision(s) of what they may be able to accomplish by working together • Assists staff in developing a shared vision of what they would like to accomplish • Gives staff an overall sense of purpose for their work
2. Models behavior	• Leads as much by "doing" as by "telling" • Symbolizes success and accomplishment within the profession • Provides good models (in addition to self) for staff to follow • Commands respect from most staff
3. Provides individualized support	• Helps staff members find resources to accomplish their professional goals • Treats staff members as individuals with unique needs and capacities • Listens carefully to individual opinions when initiating actions which affect their work • Thoughtful of personal needs of staff members

Variables and Indicators for District and School Leadership	Illustrative Measures
4. Provides intellectual stimulation	• Challenges staff to reexamine basic assumptions about their work • Stimulates staff to consider how they are contributing to district/school missions and goals • Provides information to staff to help them carry out their tasks more effectively • Provides for extended training of staff to develop their job-relevant knowledge and skill
5. Fosters commitment to group goals	• Encourages staff to work for same goals • Helps staff develop consensus around district and school priorities • Helps school staffs develop school goals consistent with district goals • Helps school staffs appreciate district mission and goals • Encourages staff to regularly monitor progress toward group goals
6. Encourages high performance expectations	• Insists on only the best performance from staff • Will not settle for second best • Assists staff to feel and act like leaders
7. Visibly acknowledges good work	• Frequently acknowledges good performance • Compliments individuals for outstanding work • Publicly recognizes exceptional effort
8. Strongly encourages individual improvement	• Encourages staff to continually strive to be better • Provides individuals with the information they need to improve their own capacity • Encourages people to take initiative

INSTRUCTIONAL SERVICES

Instructional services are obviously at the heart of a school's and district's reason for being. For the most part, the value of other variables in the district monitoring system is to be judged by the support they provide for instruction. Nevertheless, the treatment of instructional services in this chapter is relatively brief; it is a prime candidate for more intensive monitoring should the evidence collected in rela-tion to limited indicators included in the district monitoring system be cause for concern.

Although treated briefly, the variables and indicators included in the monitoring system touch on what, from our analysis of the appropriate literature, seem to be the most crucial aspects of effective instructional services, including the following:

- A constructivist view of the learning process and its implications for instruction, in particular to accomplish relatively complex goals (e.g., Cohen et al., 1993; Prawat & Peterson, 1999)
- Earlier research carrying the label of "effective teaching" and its consequent model of direct instruction, which remains viable in relation to the teaching of basic math and language skills (e.g., Brophy & Good, 1986; Peterson, 1979). This model places special emphasis on instructional time (time on task, academic learning time, etc.) as a key aspect of instruction (e.g., Rosenshine, 1979; Walberg, 1986)
- The need to align curricular goals with content and the objectives for student assessment (Murnane & Levy, 1996)
- The importance of carefully selected curricular content on the common-sense grounds that students learn what they are taught (e.g., Barr & Dreeben, 1983; Grossman, Wilson & Shulman, 1989)
- Organization of instruction to accomplish more complex goals that is less teacher directed, involving the heterogeneous grouping of students as part of various "cooperative learning" strategies (e.g., Gamoran & Berends, 1987; Slavin, 1987)
- The need for teachers to have a large repertoire of instructional strategies that they are able to use flexibly in response to the complex and unpredictable challenges that arise in the classroom (e.g., Joyce & Weil, 1972; Kagan, 1988)

Variables, indicators, and measures of instructional services included in the district monitoring system are as follows:

VARIABLES AND INDICATORS FOR INSTRUCTIONAL SERVICES	ILLUSTRATIVE MEASURES
1. Instruction is carefully planned.	• Teachers plan collaboratively for horizontal and vertical integration of objectives and content. • A clear framework is established for pursuing themes and sub-themes and for the use of individual and small group activities. • Provision is made for diverse student experiences.
2. Instructional goals are appropriate and clear.	• Instructional goals, content, and the focus of student assessment are carefully aligned. • Goals are compatible with school, district, and provincial/state goals and priorities. • Students are assisted in developing a clear understanding of the purposes for instruction.

Variables and Indicators for Instructional Services	Illustrative Measures
3. Instructional content is challenging.	• Subject matter content is selected on the basis of its authentic reflection of appropriate academic discipline, relevance to students' interests, and stage in students' development.
4. Instructional strategies are suited to instructional objectives and students' needs.	• Teachers are skilled in the use of a large repertoire of instructional strategies. • Teachers establish a relaxed, engaging physical and social environment that minimizes distractions from the purposes for instruction. • Students' opportunities to construct their own knowledge are maximized; time spent passively "absorbing" knowledge is kept to a minimum.

5. Instructional strategies reflect defensible principles of learning.	• There is evidence, in the classroom of
	  - cooperative activity, extensive interaction
	  - use of factual questions to establish a foundation followed by higher-order questions requiring more interpretation
	  - discussions kept very concrete
	  - demonstrations of relevance of curriculum to everyday world of students
	  - techniques for involving them in relevant activities
	  - fairly rapid pace of instruction
	  - limited focus within a single "lesson"
	  - actively structured and directed classroom activity

6. Instructional time is used effectively.	• Time lost to absenteeism and lateness is kept to minimum. • Classes begin promptly • Transition times are kept to a minimum • Student behavior is managed in such a way as to minimize disruptions during class • Time on task is consistently high

✳ ✳ ✳ ✳ ✳ ✳

SUMMARY   Appendixes A and B include seven short surveys of the processes described in this chapter. There are separate district and school surveys for each of planning, managing, and leading. In addition, there is a survey for describing classroom instructional services.

Structure and Organization, Information Collection and Decision Making

This chapter provides justification for two aspects of district and school characteristics, conditions and processes; structures and organization, and information collection and decision-making processes. Also described are the associated variables, indicators, and measures included in the monitoring system.

I can think of the discipline committee that I am on. It started off . . . with a bunch of us seeing that things were getting a little slack in terms of some of the issues we wanted to address. One of the teachers then formed a committee. I hesitate to say that she took a leadership role, but she is the one who initiated it; those people who were interested joined and started an informal discussion. I think that is how most of the things happen here.

Informally, I would say once a week we meet as a team and go out for lunch. We chat about things every day but we really don't talk about the program until we sit down at our Friday lunch. So this gives us about three to four hours once a month for real decision making.

STRUCTURE AND ORGANIZATION

Both of these quotations are from teachers (involved in one of our studies) responding to questions about how important decisions are made in their schools: the first, a secondary teacher; the second a primary teacher. Both teachers worked in schools that were moving quickly and with apparent success to implement selected aspects of new province-wide curriculum frameworks. The more complete responses from which these quotes were excerpted suggest that the success experienced by these schools was, in no small measure, due to the nature of how they were structured and organized for decision making.

In Chapter 3, we argued that a district or school's organization and decision-making structures have a substantial influence on their flexibility. More centralized, hierarchical structures are often efficient for reinforcing past behavior and ensuring the reliable performance of routines. Such structures, however, are not well suited to the adaptation of organizational practices. Decentralized structures, in contrast, encourage learning and reflective action-taking. They do this by spreading, to multiple members of the organization, the demands for thinking about new information. This reduces the cognitive workload of individuals, making it easier for them to assimilate those new patterns of practice.

The two quotations beginning this section help to illustrate the form that decentralized structures may take. They also hint at the investment staff members develop in school problem solving in the contexts of these structures and the opport-unities created for significant learning. These are the primary objectives to be met in structuring and organizing districts and schools so as to foster organizational learning.

The variables, indicators and measures of district structure and organization included in the monitoring system are as follows:

VARIABLES AND INDICATORS FOR DISTRICT STRUCTURE AND ORGANIZATION	ILLUSTRATIVE MEASURES

1. Engages in continuous efforts to find the most productive locus for decision making.	• Evidence of a plan for decentralization that includes:
	  - stages of exploration, trial, and commitment
	  - clarification of decisions to be decentralized
	  - assessment of breadth of support for further decentralization
	  - monitoring of impact of decentralization
	    a) flexibility of school decision making
	    b) accountability of schools
	    c) productivity
	  - review and revision periodically

2. Organizational structures facilitate day-to-day work of staff.	• Teachers, administrators, and support staff perceive organizational structures to be helpful to their work from day to day.
3. Organizational structures facilitate organizational learning and long-term problem-solving capacity.	• Staff perceive encouragement to collaborate with others from the same, as well as from different, areas of the organization (team approach). • Staff perceive opportunities for frequent, "dense" communication with other members of organization. • Staff do not perceive organization to be "over-bureaucratized."
4. Collateral or parallel groups are established to foster development of alternative points of view; these may be ad hoc groups sometimes.	• Staff perceive encouragement for considering wide range of practices and believe themselves to be involved with others in considering such practices.
5. Large districts take initiatives designed to minimize the typically negative effects on a wide variety of outputs of their large size and the large size of some of their schools.	• Evidence of substantial decentralization of decision making to schools • Evidence of support for variation in programs and other services from school to school • Evidence of each school being treated as unique, in important ways

At the school level, the monitoring system incorporates variables, indicators, and measures that overlap with many of those described at the district level. In addition, at the school level, the monitoring system speaks to the organization of students for instruction. It does this by synthesizing a large body of evidence concerning the effects on students of heterogeneous and homogeneous grouping patterns (e.g., Slavin, 1987; Gamoran, 1987; Kulik & Kulik, 1982).

VARIABLES AND INDICATORS FOR SCHOOL STRUCTURE AND ORGANIZATION	ILLUSTRATIVE MEASURES
1. School is structured and organized to support the purposes of the curriculum and requirements for instruction implied by the school's mission and goals.	• School meets all legal and contractual requirements regarding instructional time. • School day is structured for maximum instructional use. • Within the school year instructional time is maximized.
2. School is structured and organized to facilitate the professional work of teachers.	• Organization of school, timetable, etc. allows for flexible classroom-level decision making within the day. • Timetable makes provision for collaborative teacher planning time. • Realistic levels of clerical support are available to teachers.
3. Organizational structures facilitate organizational learning and long-term problem-solving capacity.	• Staff perceive that they are encouraged to collaborate with others. • Staff perceive easy access to ideas from outside the school. • Quality time is available for discussion to assist in making new ideas meaningful.
4. School structure encourages teacher collaboration, initiative, and leadership for the purpose of maximizing student learning opportunities.	• Staff perceive that school structures support teacher collaboration, initiative, and leadership for the purpose of maximizing student learning opportunities.

5. Students are organized within and across classes so as to nurture both achievement and equity goals.	• Heterogeneous grouping of students within and across classes is the norm.
	• Homogeneous grouping of students:
	  - is limited to a small proportion of any student's schedule
	  - is provided to high-achieving students in one or two areas of especially high-aptitude or interest
	  - is provided to low achieving students only in those cases in which they experience special difficulty
	• Procedures for allocating students to a homogeneous group
	  - are clearly understood and shared in common by all those involved in the allocation decision
	  - involve only criteria specifically related to the instructional purposes of the grouping arrangement
	  - incorporate explicit checks against bias in allocation decisions based on social status, ethnicity, gender, and other qualities that challenge the equity of the allocation

- provide for frequent review of allocation decisions and reallocation as appropriate
- When homogeneous grouping is appropriate, especially for low achieving groups of students, steps are taken to
    - allocate more than average instructional resources
    - specifically adapt instruction to the needs of the group
    - ensure that there is no erosion in the quality of the academic content of programs

INFORMATION COLLECTION AND DECISION-MAKING PROCESSES

My answers reflect a lack of knowledge, understanding and guidance of "proposed" curricula of provincial /state policies and directions. Also, there is a strongly felt lack of communication between staff and administration about goals, decision-making-sharing processes, implementation of changes.

The other day, I asked for feedback from the staff on how it [a peer tutoring program] was going and what their perception of it was. We have 40 people on staff and I got feedback from 18 or 19. I fed back to them the information I got and then we engaged in an open dialogue on how things could be improved.

The school decided last year to institute an S.S.R. [silent reading program] to run each morning. It was not just a hasty decision made by a small group of people or just by the administration and then imposed. It took months and months of a committee of interested people working on it. There was a lot of input like surveys; questions; the kids were surveyed. It was almost too much; it was almost too slow. Eventually, when it finally started last fall, nobody could say that their voice had not been heard. The thing was examined thoroughly and done very well.

"Garbage in, garbage out" is an adage sometimes used in the context of statistical data analysis: No amount of sophistication in statistical analysis will compensate for information collected poorly in the first place. Something similar is true of organizational learning in schools and districts. The

The quality of that learning depends significantly on (a) the amount and quality of information available to members of the organization to assist in their learning and (b) the methods used for processing that information.

quality of that learning depends significantly on (a) the amount and quality of information available to members of the organization to assist in their learning and (b) the methods used for processing that information.

The quotations opening this chapter are all from secondary school teachers in response to questions about school decision making in the context of government initiatives. Their responses illustrate a range of approaches a school might take to information collection and decision making. The first teacher's response indicates that apparently little or no information was made available to the teacher by the school; as the surrounding text indicated, this resulted in feelings of confusion and hostility on the part of the teacher and no learning that was likely to improve the teacher's practices. Furthermore, the teacher's remarks suggest little or no participation in decision making about how to respond to government initiatives.

The second and third quotations are in stark contrast to the first, indicating highly participative forms of decision making informed by considerable amounts of carefully accumulated data. The second teacher describes how this can be done quite nimbly; the process described by the third teacher is clearly more protracted, perhaps even ponderous in her view, but likely useful in the long term, nonetheless.

Learning organizations behave in ways nicely illustrated by the second and third quotations (Louis & Kruse, 1998). Obviously, having access to relevant information expands decision alternatives and provides a firmer basis for choosing among those alternatives. The participation of all relevant stakeholders assumes that many heads are capable of better sense-making than one is.

Variables, indicators, and measures of district-level information collection and decision making included in the monitoring system are as follows:

VARIABLES AND INDICATORS FOR DISTRICT INFORMATION COLLECTION AND DECISION-MAKING PROCESSES	ILLUSTRATIVE MEASURES
1. Collects optimum amounts and types of information	• Evidence of systematic, district-wide student assessment program • Evidence of systematic monitoring of progress with school improvement plans
2. Makes effective use of information for decision making	• Incorporates student assessment data into all appropriate decisions • Provides principals with variety of school-specific information, which is discussed and expectations for use established
3. Makes effective use of information for organizational learning	• Undistorted horizontal and vertical communication with sharing of relevant facts and feelings • Fosters flow of ideas into and throughout district • Ample opportunities for integrating knowledge across informal groups and for the "social interpretation" of information

VARIABLES AND INDICATORS FOR DISTRICT INFORMATION COLLECTION AND DECISION-MAKING PROCESSES	ILLUSTRATIVE MEASURES
4. Uses productive forms of decision making and problem solving	• All stakeholder groups participate in significant district-level decisions • Decision making takes place nearest the source of best information, regardless of source • District mission and goals used as criteria for decision making • Adoption of a longer term perspective for decision making than just the annual cycle • Procedures for decision making are perceived to be reasonable and clear
5. Nurtures a proactive attitude toward decision making and problem solving	• Problems viewed as issues to be solved or circumvented rather than barriers to action • Perception that problems may provide windows of opportunity for reaching important objectives
6. Ensures compliance of all categories of personnel with decision-making roles and responsibilities specified in relevant contracts and laws	• All categories of personnel know those requirements of their role specified in relevant contracts and laws • Supervisory staff routinely monitor knowledge and compliance of those they supervise with roles and responsibilities as specified in contracts and laws

At the school level, the monitoring system includes the following variables, indicators, and measures:

VARIABLES AND INDICATORS FOR SCHOOL INFORMATION COLLECTION AND DECISION-MAKING PROCESSES	ILLUSTRATIVE MEASURES
1. Systematic collection of information critical to school maintenance and improvement	• The school regularly collects a variety of types of data about individual student progress. • Teacher performance is monitored through regular reviews by a school administrator or peer.
2. Information is used to assist in decision-making processes that range from highly participative to autonomous, depending on the issue.	• Teachers typically participate in most significant, school-level, policy decisions (e.g., assignment of students to classes, school goals and priorities).
3. Decisions regarding the stream of problems associated with school improvement initiatives (problem coping) are distributed among many teachers and administrators are not the sole purview of the principal.	• School has established a "steering group" to manage the change process. • Most staff believe themselves to be responsible for solving implementation problems that they encounter; it is not "someone else's job."

VARIABLES AND INDICATORS FOR SCHOOL INFORMATION COLLECTION AND DECISION-MAKING PROCESSES	ILLUSTRATIVE MEASURES
4. School staff recognizes decisions about which it needs assistance and seeks such assistance.	• Staff recognize their limitations and are open to assistance from those external to the school. • School co-opts external expertise for support in problem solving and in training.
5. Student assessment practices in the classroom yield valid and reliable information.	• Student progress is monitored frequently. • There is a good match between program goals and the focus of student assessment. • A variety of assessment information is collected about student progress. • Teachers have developed a high level of consensus about criteria and standards.
6. Student assessment information collected in the classroom is used to improve instruction.	• Teachers are able to assess the presence of student misconceptions and have ways of overcoming them during instruction. • Student assessment results are used to plan future instruction. • Students are given specific feedback about their learning. • Students are rewarded for significant achievement.

❊ ❊ ❊ ❊ ❊ ❊

The two sets of variables described in this chapter play key "supporting" roles in organizational learning. Structure and organization create opportunities for people to think together—or prevent such thinking from taking place—depending on their nature. Information collection and decision-making processes provide much of the fuel and mechanisms for use in such thinking. As schools and districts move from less to more inclusive structures and organization, and from poorer to better quality information for decision making, organizational learning increasingly will be fostered.

SUMMARY

Chapter 9

Policies and Procedures, Community Partnerships

This chapter describes the orientation of the monitoring system toward the final two school and district processes encompassed within it.

POLICIES AND PROCEDURES

Several of [the district initiatives] are very good and are ideal, but then so were aspects of communism. Making it work in practice and having it be a beautiful ideal are two different things.

District-level initiative has already died. Committee formation [is] ignored by secondary teachers; teachers want a very specific instruction outline: "What do you want me to teach, with what students, and how?" Ministry/state guidelines are either vague or impossible.

What I teach in the classroom is driven by curriculum. We can delete or add as we see fit, but certainly the curriculum is the guide. I do personal professional development by going to workshops, science workshops, or conferences. But the school-based professional development is not curriculum oriented.

The principal and the vice principal were very careful when they did their hiring to select people with the same sort of philosophies, the same sort of ideas, and they had us all get together last June, they had us get together in April, May, picking materials, looking at our different resources, planning what we would like in our classrooms; so they pulled us together way before the full year even started.

These teachers' comments illustrate a variety of responses to restructuring policy (the first two), a variety of expectations for policy (the second and third) and a variety of beliefs about their productive use in school improvement (the last). The first quotation exemplifies a view of *policy as sometimes unworkable philosophy*. From this view it is possible, at the same time, to agree with a philosophy (or policy) and to continue with practices not supported by the philosophy. Schön (1987) describes this apparent paradox as a gap between espoused theory and theory-in-use, and Senge (1990) argues that until the gap is overcome, significant learning is unlikely to occur. This unlikelihood is so because such a gap probably indicates only surface understanding of the espoused theory; it is also probably symptomatic of a much more deeply understood but unrecognized theory actually guiding one's practices. Learning organizations help members discover their theories-in-use. They also help members compare those theories with members' espoused theories and theories espoused by themselves, others, and by policy. As a consequence, the gap is likely to be reduced and policies become real guides to action.

The second quotation illustrates two matters of importance in the development of learning organizations. First, policies and procedures serve symbolic as well as more instrumental purposes: the death of district level "initiatives" (i.e., procedures) signifies to this teacher lack of commitment by the district to the implementation of state-wide initiatives. As a consequence, in this teacher's view, commitment to the effort on the part of his or her colleagues has also dissipated. District policies and procedures indicate to staff indirectly and symbolically, as well as directly, what learning is of most worth to the district.

District policies and procedures indicate to staff indirectly and symbolically, as well as directly, what learning is of most worth to the district.

The second quotation also illustrates a view of *policy as specifications for action*. This teacher complains of vagueness, of no specifications of when, who, or how. It is a complaint founded on assumptions: about the role of teacher as tech-nician; about the classroom as a predictable environment for instruction; and about solutions to problems of improvement as already discovered but not yet disseminated. These assumptions are untenable in a learning organization simply because they suggest that learning is somebody else's responsibility. Learning organizations encourage their members to give up such assumptions and pursue, instead, the goal of personal mastery. They do this in part by using "least restrictive" criteria in the development of policies and by ensuring coherence between policies and organizational mission: this is also done by enacting policies that directly enhance opportunities for organizational learning.

The last two quotations illustrate the potential of school-level policies and procedures to either serve the functions of school improvement quite directly or be, at best, tangential to them. The final quotation illustrates direct, instrumental use of policy for improvement purposes, whereas the third quotation illustrates how school-based professional development policies can miss the opportunity of being more directly useful.

Included in the monitoring system are variables, indicators, and measures of school and district policy that acknowledge the conditions of organizational learning reflected in the four quotations as well as other policy-related characteristics identified in our review of research.

VARIABLES AND INDICATORS FOR DISTRICT POLICIES AND PROCEDURES	ILLUSTRATIVE MEASURES
1. Orientation of policies and procedures maintains a balance between district control and school autonomy.	• Clear rules and guidelines provided by district which schools are encouraged to implement flexibly • Avoidance of excessive paper work in schools • Considerable opportunity for school input into policies, discretion in their implementation but considerable district control over goals and assessment of their accomplishment
2. Policies and procedures, as a whole, support the accomplishment of district and school goals.	• Staff goals not allowed to displace student goals but recognition of, and attention to, staff needs • Policies and procedures are aligned with district and school mission and goals (coherent) • Policies and procedures do not contradict one another (consistent)
3. District personnel devote special attention to policies and procedures governing areas especially key to accomplishing district goals. These areas will depend, to some extent, on district goals. Some likely areas to consider in most districts include, for example:	
3.1 Staff development	• District-sponsored staff development directly reflects district goals • On- and off-site assistance provided to teachers and administrators • Broad range of staff development opportunities available • Release time available for staff development

3.2 Administrator (and teacher) evaluation	• District policy reflects a commitment to growth based on clear criteria that:
	   a) are tied to district and school goals; and
	   b) are consistent with research on effective practice.
	Administrators are rewarded for fostering the growth of teachers and other administrators and for creating effective work groups.
	• Evidence about performance is based on several forms of information, collected regularly.
	• Collective bargaining agreements reflect a priority for growth.
	• Time is appropriated for the conferencing, observation, and feedback needed to produce improvements.
	• Resources are made available for evaluation

Variables and Indicators for District Policies and Procedures	Illustrative Measures

	• Evaluators are perceived to be
	  - a credible source of sound ideas
	  - persuasive on reasons for change
	  - patient with regard to change
	  - worthy of trust
	  - able to model/demonstrate needed change

3.3 Program, curriculum, and instruction	• District has established instructional goals, district-wide. • Policies encourage teachers to acquire a large repertoire of instructional strategies, and they choose strategies based on instructional goals and student characteristics.
3.4 School improvement	• Clear guidelines are provided to schools regarding benchmarks. • School planning process is mandated for all schools. • Schools demonstrate connection between their plans and the directions of the district.

At the school level, variables, indicators, and measures included in the monitoring system are as follows:

Variables and Indicators for School Policies and Procedures	Illustrative Measures
1. Policies and procedures, as a whole, support accomplishment of school's goals.	• Policies and procedures are aligned with school goals (coherent). • Policies and procedures do not contradict one another (consistent).
2. Student-oriented policies emphasize student achievement.	• Policies encourage high standards of student work. • A student assessment policy is in place. • Policies require homework to be regularly assigned and graded or commented on (especially intermediate and graduating levels).
3. Student-oriented policies minimize disruptive behavior.	• Simple, clear standards and rules for students are developed. • Students and parents participate in establishing behavior standards and rules. • Exemplary student behavior is valued and rewarded.
4. Student-oriented policies provide for students with special needs.	• School is moving away from pull-out programs and toward meeting special student needs in regular classes.
5. Student-oriented policies foster students' sense of affiliation with the school.	• Ensure access to counselors at intermediate and graduating levels. • Students provided with a pleasant, comfortable environment. • Opportunities for students to take responsibility and participate in running the school.

VARIABLES AND INDICATORS FOR DISTRICT POLICIES AND PROCEDURES	ILLUSTRATIVE MEASURES
6. Teacher-oriented policies encourage staff experience, academic competence, and stability.	• Selection policies favor a high proportion of staff with five or more years experience, with higher levels of attainment in their specialities, often with advanced degrees. • Staff supervision is collaborative, linked to school goals, and provides for staff development. • Staff stability is normally encouraged.

7. Staff development policies encourage continuous growth as well as attention to shorter-term needs.	• Resources available for school-based staff development (time, money)
	• Such activity
	  - is focused and coordinated
	  - is defined at school level, often
	  - centers on school and classroom practices teachers perceive to be significant
	  - includes follow-up, collegial assistance and evaluation
	• Incorporates relevant, research-based knowledge
	• Designed around principles of adult learning
	• May take a range of formal to informal forms
	• Special training provided to teachers in those instructional techniques specifically for use with heterogeneous groups of students

8. Resources are allocated to reinforce school goals and priorities but without stifling individual initiative	• Allocation of a large proportion of discretionary resources is aligned with school goals. • Teachers have access to discretionary funds to support their own improvement initiatives. • Additional assistance is provided to teachers responsible for classes with unusually wide ranges of student ability.

DISTRICT- AND SCHOOL-COMMUNITY PARTNERSHIPS

[The community is] growing uncomfortably fast in that . . . the districts have a hard time keeping up financially with the number of children coming in. The city has had a hard time keeping up road structures and design. . . . They don't design an intersection properly because it's fine for a month before they build it, and then the month or two after they build it, it no longer works properly because the population has changed so much in between. . . . This community is expected to double in the next seven years.

The school is held in fairly high regard and has good support in the community. If a group of teachers wanted to take on something that could be justified and was not totally off the wall, I am sure the community would be all behind it. If it was about a new initiative in the school, there would be no problem in obtaining the support of the community. It is a very supportive community.

*The current program has a reasonably good fit in this community.
It can be fine-tuned but should not be abandoned.*

Closer and more extensive relationships between districts, schools, and their communities is a central pillar of many current educational restructuring initiatives (e.g., Darling-Hammond, 1993). These relationships take many forms: for example, local governing councils for schools in Great Britain, which have opted out of their local educational authorities (Walford, 1993); parent-dominated decision bodies for local schools in Chicago and parts of Australia (Crowson, 1992); and various forms of parent involvement directly in student work at home and in the classroom (Lareau, 1989). Reasons for such relationships, particularly between schools and their local communities, suggested by a synthesis of recent research include (a) helping some parents improve their parenting skills and foster conditions in the home that support learning, (b) providing parents with knowledge of educational techniques to assist children learning at home, (c) increasing accountability, and (d) providing access to and coordinating community and support services for children and families. Closer school-community relationships are also intended to promote clear two-way communication between the school and the family regarding school programs and student progress; involve parents in instructional support roles at school; support parents as decision makers and develop their leadership in governance, advisory, and advocacy roles; and use community resources and opportunities to strengthen the school program.

At the district level, closer relationships with the community are strongly linked to the maintenance of political support for the school and its financial demands as well as ensuring appropriate links between school programs and the requirements of employers.

At the district level, closer relationships with the community are strongly linked to the maintenance of political support for the school and its financial demands as well as ensuring appropriate links between school programs and the requirements of employers. The first quotation opening this section provides blunt illustration of how something as straightforward as changing community demographics can have dramatic consequences for such things as school building. Demographic changes are likely to be accompanied also by more subtle changes in community values, family educational cultures, employer expectations, social aspirations, and the like. To maintain a school district sensitive to such obvious and not so obvious changes requires quite close district-community relationships. Much less evidence is available, however, about productive district, as compared with school-community relationships.

In the case of both schools and districts, community relationships may be developed in ways that foster organizational learning. Teachers, for example, often express apprehension about greater parent participation in school (Lareau, 1989). Indeed, the second quotation opening this section encompasses most teachers' perspectives on the ideal form of school-parent relationship — interested, generally supportive, but at arm's length. The third quotation illustrates, however, the sensitivity many teachers have to the power of parents over school decisions on those still relatively rare occasions when parents see something in their local school to which they object.

Yet parents are a rich source of information about the instructional needs of their students, sometimes able to predict school conditions which foster student learning better than teachers (Snydor & Ebmeier, 1992). Parents also bring fresh perspectives to the school about priorities for education and more specific causes of students' responses to instruction.

Variables, indicators, and measures of district-community relationships warranted by available evidence are quite limited. These include the following:

VARIABLES AND INDICATORS FOR DISTRICT-COMMUNITY PARTNERSHIPS	ILLUSTRATIVE MEASURES
1. District is "at peace" with larger community; has created or nurtured acceptance of district activities. Although sometimes active, generally this acceptance is passive.	• Local newspapers print positive stories about system. • Absence of strong, negative, vocal advocacy groups • Existence of cooperative ventures between schools and district and businesses
2. District communicates mission and goals to community in many formal and informal ways: builds public confidence, support, and a sense of partnership.	• Publication of strategic plan • Speaking at service clubs and in other public forums about district's goals and plans • Providing public with avenues for authentic input into district decisions • Attention to a variety of media and to segmenting audiences with targeted material

At the school level, the monitoring system includes the following school-community variables, indicators, and measures:

VARIABLES AND INDICATORS FOR SCHOOL-COMMUNITY PARTNERSHIPS	ILLUSTRATIVE MEASURES
1. School has developed productive relationships with the business/industry sector of the local community.	• Members of business/industry are used as specialized resources in the regular curriculum. • Business/industry demonstrate cooperation in implementing such things as co-op programs, work-experience, and mentorships. • Business/industry demonstrate willingness to sponsor special projects. • Minimal public criticism, by members of business and industry is directed at schools (e.g., in newspapers).
2. School has developed productive relationships with the postsecondary sector of the local community.	• Postsecondary faculty are used as specialized resources in the regular curriculum. • Postsecondary institutions provide assistance in the enrichment of programs for academically talented students.
3. School has incorporated parents into the school's programs as partners in the education of their children.	• School promotes clear, two-way communication between school and family regarding school programs and student progress. • Teachers establish good relationships with parents, directly and actively encourage interaction between parents and selves • Support parents as decision makers in the school and help develop their leadership in governance, advisory, and advocacy roles, using such structures as parent advisory councils, for example • Involve parents, after appropriate training, in instructional and support roles in classroom and school • Develop high levels of parental support for school initiatives
4. School collaborates with parents in the development of a productive educational culture in the home.	• School encourages the availability of programs (not necessarily by direct provision) to develop parenting skills, where there is a need. • Encourages parent involvement in children's homework
5. School has developed productive relationships with the community at large.	• Provides access to and coordinates community and support services for children and families, as needed • There are positive reports about schools and minimal public criticism in the media. • Demonstrated willingness to provide further funding for schools when asked (e.g., referenda)

✳ ✳ ✳ ✳ ✳ ✳

SUMMARY

Policies and procedures serve the explicit purpose of guiding the decisions and actions of district and school personnel; they also convey implicit, symbolic information about what the district and school values are, and hence, what is important to learn. So the monitoring system assesses not only the perceived content of school and district policies but also their effects on staff beliefs about priorities for their work.

Partnerships between school/district and community are to be nurtured as sources of support for educators' work in schools, as ways of effectively extending the educational program of the school into the family, and as a means of enriching the school's contribution to student growth. The extent to which each of these purposes for district/school-community partnerships is being achieved is assessed by the monitoring system.

PART IV: GATHERING AND USING SCHOOL AND DISTRICT MONITORING INFORMATION

The aspects of the district monitoring system described so far have concerned what information to collect and why. We have also alluded to Appendixes A and B, which contain survey instruments to assist in such information collection. But if you like what you have read so far, you will have accumulated many practical questions about just how to use the monitoring system. Chapters 10 and 11 provide guidelines for increasing the chances that schools and districts will actually use and learn from monitoring-system information. As Madau and Tan (1993) said in their reference to student test data, "It is not the form of the tests . . . that is important in determining the impact of a testing program on students, teachers and schools. Instead, it is the use to which the results are put" (p. 73). The same can be said for monitoring-system information. Its use will determine the text to which the monitoring system truly does make schools and districts smarter.

Chapter 10

Collecting, Analyzing, and Interpreting Monitoring Information

As Bryk and Hermanson (1993) mentioned in Chapter 1, the ultimate test of the monitoring system is that it should help us act more prudently, not simply inform us better. But to act wisely, we need information. This chapter describes how the monitoring system might be used to acquire data, turn it into useful information, and eventually into strategies for action. Primarily, this chapter is concerned with data arising from surveys, like those included in Appendixes A and B, about school and district processes—those features discussed in detail in Chapters 6 through 9. Also touched on, however, is the analysis and use of data that many schools and districts regularly collect or acquire about inputs and outcomes.

In setting out this discussion, a distinction is made between "comprehensive" and "strategic" monitoring. We draw on our experience with the monitoring system in several hundred schools in three large districts to illustrate how the system can be used with good effect.

This treatment of data collection and analysis is neither sophisticated nor a replacement for more technically oriented advice. It is, rather, a primer of issues that require attention and a description of some options for approaching these issues. A school or district with access to an evaluation specialist would not likely find this chapter of great use.

The chapter is organized into three parts, as its title suggests. In the collecting part, survey development and administration are discussed—some basics of good survey design and sampling in nontechnical language. In the analyzing part, methods for organizing data are discussed. In the interpreting part, the process that we have used with schools and districts is described—not because it is the only process available, but because it provided for the significant involvement of many members of the school district's constituencies and had encouraging effects.

Chapters 6 through 9 described critical variables or features of districts and schools. Indicators defining these variables were identified, as were measures to determine the extent to which these variables were present in a school and district.

COLLECTING

We began with a lengthy list of possible measures for each variable indicator and then reduced and refined these to develop the surveys included in Appendixes A and B. All of these surveys are, of course, provided for schools and districts to use, adapt, or reject as they see fit. Whether schools and districts use these in some form or develop their own, a number of things should be kept in mind, as discussed below.

Constituent Participation in Development

For a number of obvious, and some less than obvious, reasons, representatives of all school or district constituencies should participate in the development or the review and modification of data-gathering instruments:

- The greater the degree of participation, the greater the stake in the results.
- If those who are to respond to the instrument have a hand in its development or refinement, they will not only willingly answer the questions but also urge their colleagues to do likewise.
- Each constituency best knows what questions it should be asked and would like to be asked.
- Because politics (with a small "p") is an ever-present dimension of a district's or school's operating context, decisions are more likely to be influenced by data gathered, interpreted, and formulated into recommendations from a large representation of constituencies.
- If the populations to be sampled are the same populations that comprise the reality of the school or district (employees, students, parents), then they should be part of the data-gathering design.
- The ideal school and district, as we have been saying all along, is collaborative, shares its decision making, and locates the decisions closest to the point of their greatest impact.

Where we have been asked to help schools and districts use the monitoring system, representative committes of teachers, principals, central office administrators, and sometimes support staff have been created. Their tasks have included the following:

- Modifying the surveys (Appendixes A and B) to better reflect their own context
- Deciding on the most acceptable procedures for distributing and collecting data
- Communicating with their colleagues about the procedures and explaining the importance of the data collection activities

If you wish to modify the existing surveys in Appendixes A and B, replace them with your own, or add something more specific to your particular needs, some general guidelines about designing surveys are worth reviewing briefly here.

- *Determine the goals and objectives* for your survey (what you want to know in broad and specific terms).
- *Identify the variables* (a characteristic or attribute of persons, objects, or events that differs in value across such persons, objects, or events) than can be influenced by educational action (e.g., district mission and goals).
- *Agree which indicators should be measured.* The indicators being measured in the survey of district mission and goals are Clarity, Meaningfulness, Awareness, and Usefulness.
- *Draft the measures to reference the indicators.*
- *Word the questions clearly and simply* (also remember the rules of grammar and diction; for instance, use parallelism, when it is called for).
- *Ensure that the question or item addresses only one indicator.*
- *Consider carefully the order in which you place the questions* (it is best to move from specific to general judgment on what they have said about more specific issues).
- *Pilot-test the items* so that you can be sure the questions are eliciting reliable and valid responses.
- *Consider carefully the measurement scale* you should employ.

Survey Design

People generally do one of three things when they receive survey results: (a) Accept them if they like the results, (b) attack their reliability and validity if they do not like what they say, or (c) begin to think about why the results appear to say what they do.

More detailed sources of information about these and other relevant guidelines can be found in *Survey Research Methods* (Fowler, 1988), *How to Measure Attitudes* (Henerson, 1987), and *How to Analyze Data* (FitzGibbon, 1987). The more careful and painstaking the "upfront" time spent in designing the survey, the fewer the problems that arise later, when one is reporting the results. People generally do one of three things when they receive survey results: (a) Accept them if they like the results, (b) attack their reliability and validity if they do not like what they say, or (c) begin to think about why the results appear to say what they do. The last of these reactions is the most productive, so whatever can be done to ensure the reliability and validity of results should be done.

If the monitoring system is used in an individual school, sampling is not a very complicated matter. Very likely all teachers, administrators, and support staff would be asked to provide information; student data may

Sampling

already be on file. So parents are the only group that may need special planning. If, however, the monitoring system is being used across a district, sampling decisions can be a challenge. Here are some rules of thumb to keep in mind.

Determine respondent populations. In the original field test of the monitoring system, all constituencies in one district participated: employees, students, and parents. For each survey, we had to determine which group should and would respond. We included all of the respondent groups: teachers, administrators, support staff, parents, and trustees. We had students respond only to the participation and identification survey, but were we to do it again, we would have members of the student consultative committee and perhaps the student councils they represent respond to all surveys where they could reasonably be expected to have legitimate opinions. It is important, then, that the survey section requesting background information provide spaces for respondents to indicate their role. Also, one of the things we learned the hard way is to remind respondents at the end of the survey to make sure they complete the respondent role section. We forgot to do this in the field test and consequently had a large "other" group.

Notice that we did not separate our support staff by subcategory. Determining the category level at which to leave the designator is more a matter of being able to show differences without identifying individuals or promoting unwanted comparisons.

Obtain a representative sample. We think that, for small populations such as trustees or secondary school administrators, all should be surveyed. For a school of 300 students, it would be wise to survey all teachers and probably 20% to 30% of the parents, at the very least. If it will not cost significantly more time and money to survey all parents, then do so. "The smaller the population, the larger the sample needed to represent the potential variance" is a good rule of thumb. If the population is very large (e.g., all parents in the district), a sufficient number of all subgroups (e.g., parents of primary students, parents in the west end of the district as opposed to the east, parents who are active in parent councils and those who are not) must be included—stratify the sample, in other words.

The size of the sample will also be influenced by the cost of analyzing the results. If the jurisdiction has access to electronic scanning, larger numbers of returns can be read at little added cost. The cost per instrument of producing the surveys themselves usually decreases as the numbers increase.

The major issue in the sample size is the likely return rate. If the return rate is going to be low, one would be wise to survey such a large number that the results will not be attacked as completely nonrepresentative. A number of things encourage a high return rate: (a) participation in the design and review by the respondents or a credible subset of them, (b) encouragement by the executives of teacher associations/unions to their membership to respond, (c) preliminary knowledge of what the survey is intended to do for the participants in the short and long run, (d) assurance of the opportunity to participate in interpreting and using the results, (e) assurance that the survey does not demand too much time to complete, and, most important, (f) assurance that participants will have access to the results, and (g) supervised common completion time such as a staff meeting.

The major issue in the sample size is the likely return rate.

Nineteen surveys are provided in Appendixes A and B. Figure 10.1 lists the titles of these surveys, the number of items in each one, and the internal reliability of the scales formed by the items in that survey. This reliability information arises from data selected in the 120 schools of the most recent district we were asked to assist in using the monitoring system. The survey measuring immediate outcomes and one input (family educational culture) assesses the status of five related variables. To minimize systematic response bias, items measuring different aspects of these variables are not obvious from the instrument itself. So, those interpreting survey responses need to know which items are intended to form subscales measuring each variable addressed by the instrument.

Surveys Available

Many people working in schools and district offices are experienced in ensuring that directions are clear about how to respond and how to return completed surveys. They also know how best to distribute surveys to the desired respondents. Nevertheless, we present a few words of additional advice about collection strategies.

Distributing, Administering, and Collecting

- *It is crucial to develop a procedure,* prior to survey distribution, that will allow grouping of responses in the most useful categories of respondents.
- *A timeline is vital*—when surveys are to be sent out, how long for completion, and when they are to be returned.
- *Anonymity normally should be guaranteed for individual respondents.*

FIGURE 10.1. Titles and Numbers of Items in Each Survey

Questionnaires Relating to District Characteristics and Conditions

		Items	Reliability/Alpha
2.1	District Mission and Goals	18	.956
2.2	District Culture	27	.975
2.3a	District Core Tasks (a)—Planning	45	.975
2.3b	District Core Tasks (b)—Management	20	.975
2.3c	District Core Tasks (c)—Leadership	35	.956
2.4	District Structure and Organization	34	.927
2.5	District Information Collection and Decision Making	23	.936
2.6	District Policies and Procedures	37	.951
2.7	District-Community Partnerships	16	.870

Questionnaires Relating to School Characteristics and Conditions

		Items	Reliability/Alpha
3.1	School Mission and Goals	30	.974
3.2	School Culture	30	.917
3.3a	School Core Tasks (a)—Leadership	32	.978
3.3b	School Core Tasks (b)—Management	21	.938
3.3c	School Core Tasks (c)—Planning	33	.954
3.3d	School Core Tasks (d)—Instructional Services	24	.912
3.4	School Structure and Organization	26	.924
3.5	School Information Collecting and Decision Making	26	.938
3.6	School Policies and Procedures	45	.942
3.7	School-Community Partnerships	25	.948

Questionnaire Relating to Immediate Outcomes/Inputs

		Items	Reliability/Alpha
4.1	Participation in School Activities	25	.655
4.2	Identification With School	17	.814
4.3	Family Educational Culture	10	.807
4.4	Quality of Instruction	13	.878
4.5	Academic Self-Efficacy	5	.779

- *Returns should be carefully sorted* as they come in (e.g., respondent group, location, grade). It is so easy to lose track of where a survey came from if it is removed from its envelope or separated from others (the voice of hard-learned experience again).

- *Someone should be available to deal with problems, questions, and concerns that respondents might have.* It is for this reason that a supervised common setting is most valuable.

Collecting Information Other Than From the Surveys

Many schools and districts already have access to information about variables included in the monitoring system. There is no need to collect it again; rather, the task is to assemble it as an integral part of the monitoring-system data. These may be data about student demographics, attendance rates, parent opinion, and certainly student achievement. Often, as well, schools have ready access to information about class size, student-educator ratio, and educator certification and experience, as well as data about such specific programs as career preparation and English as a second language (ESL). Most of the conditions these data describe should also be considered for their potential influence on student outcomes.

When such data are available it will be well worth the effort to organize them in electronic management systems for easy access and update. The software should facilitate developing and printing reports customized to the requester's need. Information developed through these means can contribute as much to the monitoring system as data collected specifically in response to the monitoring-system survey.

Usually, once all data are collected, they will have to be transferred from the surveys to a computer so that the results can be processed for review. These results may be put into the computer in two ways: keyboarding or scanning. The latter is by far the faster and more economical means, particularly for a large volume. To scan them in, they first have to be printed on a scannable sheet. To scan the results, a jurisdiction must also have the equipment and expertise to do so. If it does not, outside agencies can be contracted to do the job. We do not deal here with all of the data entry issues that will need resolving to carry out this task. Suffice it to say that a bit of expert consultation will help decide the appropriate means of data entry and analysis, including timelines, questionnaire preparation, processing comments, data files, report format, and statistical software.

Analyzing and Reporting

One result of our experience in helping schools and districts use the monitoring system is a clear and easily understood form for reporting the results of data collected from a school. In this section, we illustrate the main features of such a reporting form and provide a brief description of how to read it. This reporting form assumes comprehensive use of the monitoring surveys, and some assistance to schools in both analyzing data and developing a report of results. Excerpts from the report appear as Exhibit 1 at the end of this chapter, and we describe the report section by section with reference to this exhibit.

Overview: Page 1. The overview reminds people of their work in responding to the survey, and of the different characteristics of the school about which they answered questions. The overview also delineates what they will find in the additional sections of the report.

Section 1: Pages 2 to 5. This section provides two types of information in addition to that on page 2. The first is contained in Figure 1, page 3, which reports the mean ratings of teachers on the 10 different characteristics of their school as well as an overall rating for the characteristics combined. Also, on this figure (and this is, of course, optional) for each of these ratings there is a comparison with the ratings provided by teachers in all other elementary schools in the district. These comparisons are often of considerable initial interest, but not terribly useful in the long run. The data in Figure 1 are presented as bar graphs, in combination with a reporting of mean ratings. This affords a quick, visual impression of strengths and weaknesses in the school, as reflected in the ratings by teachers. It is immediately evident, for example, that teachers are relatively positive about the instructional services delivered in the school, but not nearly so positive about the school's mission and goals or its leadership.

Figure 1 is followed by a series of ten additional bar graphs, one for each of the 10 school characteristics. We have included two of these figures in the exhibit, one for leadership (page 4) and one for instructional services (page 5) to illustrate the form of the bar graphs. Looking at Figure 4 (page 4), for example, displays results organized around the six dimensions of leadership that were measured by the leadership survey (Appendix A). In addition, there is an overall mean rating of school leadership, and all of these ratings are compared with teachers' ratings about leadership in all other elementary schools in the district.

This bar graph points to some of the more glaring concerns about school leadership—in this case, concerns about the leaders symbolizing good professional practice, providing intellectual stimulation, and assisting the staff in developing a vision and specific objectives for the school.

Figure 7 (page 5) reports the ratings of teachers on five different aspects of their own instruction. The positive nature of these results should stimulate debate about whether teachers are biased about their own work, as compared with the work of the school administrators, for example. Such discussions, in our experience, often have extremely positive consequences as teachers work to become more realistic about the quality of their instruction.

Section 2: Pages 6 to 8. This section of Exhibit 1 reports teachers' ratings on the individual items used to measure each of the characteristics and sub-characteristics of the school. The introductory page (6) outlines the information contained in this section and the process to understand it. The second page (7) in this section indicates which of the detailed survey items measured each of the components of the ten school characteristics. This is an especially useful feature when all survey items are included in this section, as they would be in a regular report. Following this are examples of the form we have used to report individual items (page 8). Included here are examples of only the items that were used to measure school leadership and instructional services. What is reported are the number of teachers (*N*) who responded to each item, their mean rating of the item, and the standard deviation (*SD*) of the ratings (that is the extent to which teachers agreed on the ratings of each item).

Additional data could be reported in subsequent sections, were it available, about, for example, parent opinion, student achievement, or student engagement (using the survey included in Appendix A).

Information collected through the monitoring system survey, especially in combination with other sources of information about student outcomes, provides the basis for quite valuable analysis beyond those displayed in Exhibit 1. Such analysis will sometimes require more data than an individual school can provide. One might, for example, combine the data of different categories of schools within a district if they were available (e.g., elementary schools, secondary school, schools serving large proportions of low SES children). The purpose for such data aggregation, in combination with the school's reading scores, for example, would be to answer such questions as: Should schools serving low SES students focus their efforts to improve reading scores on different characteristics of their organizations than schools serving middle SES students?

To illustrate some of these possibilities, we describe some analyses we undertook for one district that had collected monitoring data from all of its schools with revised versions of the surveys in Appendixes A and B. In

Additional Analyses

addition to such data about school characteristics, the district also had data about the following:

- Grade 7 math and language achievement
- Grade 12 writing achievement
- Student suspension rates in all schools
- Student engagement data (Appendix A, Survey 11) in all schools

Our analysis concentrated primarily on the relationships between variation in the rating of school characteristics and variation in student outcomes measures (correlations, regression analyses). Among the findings of these additional analyses were the following:

Grade 7 math and language. We found that for the 31 schools, their school mission and goals, school culture, and management (and leadership) contributed more than any other variables to math and language achievement. Schools in which students identified more strongly with the school also tended to be schools that scored above expectation on basic math and language skills. Furthermore, general instructional strategies, by themselves, explained about 20% of the variance in Grade 7 student math and language scores.

Suspension rates. Information about student suspension rates were available for all elementary and secondary schools. Results of the analyses showed that higher ratings on classroom instructional practices were significantly related to reduced levels of student suspension. Management was the only school-level variable significantly related to student suspensions. But the direction of the relationship was counter to expectations (i.e., higher scores on school management were related to higher levels of student suspension). Furthermore, higher levels of student achievement were significantly related to lower levels of student suspension, and higher levels of student participation were significantly but weakly associated with lower levels of student suspension. We concluded that improving classroom instruction was likely to be a much more potent, albeit indirect, strategy for reducing suspension rates than more direct efforts to manage it at the school level.

Interpreting   Interpretation is determining what the monitoring results mean. After the monitoring data are analyzed and organized to reveal patterns and relationships, each school or constituent group must determine what such information means to it in terms of decisions and actions. And, as most educators are painfully aware, the same evaluation results can mean very different things to different people. As Humpty Dumpty said, "It means just what I choose it to mean—neither more nor less." But the possibility of alternative interpretations should not be a cause for excessive hand-wringing.

Although there are many useful methods for interpreting data, all such methods share some common features:

- Involvement of those likely to be affected by the decisions arising from the results
- Clear specification of the questions to be answered as part of the interpretation process
- Consideration of the context in which the results arose
- Comparison of results with an a priori ideal or some "standard" in order to identify school or district strengths and weaknesses
- Individual interpretation first, followed by small group, and then whole group interpretation of the meaning of results
- Drafting of recommendations concerning strategic actions justified by the results and their interpretation

✳   ✳   ✳   ✳   ✳   ✳

This chapter outlined some basic procedures that could be used to collect, analyze, and interpret data arising from the administration of the 19 surveys included in Appendixes A and B. Also discussed were the data available to and collected by school districts about their inputs and outcomes. Emphasis was given to the importance of establishing an electronic data management system that allows for ongoing update, access, and reporting of data.

Application of all or a large subset of the monitoring system surveys (comprehensive monitoring) is likely to be necessary (or even feasible) once every 3 to 4 years. Results emerging from such application will suggest specific actions that, together with shifts in priorities, may necessitate more in-depth data collection about selected issues (strategic monitoring). Comprehensive and strategic monitorings each have their own purposes and may follow one on the other over time.

SUMMARY

Exhibit 10.1   Excerpts From A Model Report of Survey Results: Pine Hill Elementary School

Overview

Earlier this year, teachers responded to a survey concerning different aspects of the school. As well, a sample of students was asked about the extent and nature of their participation and identification with the school.

Information collected through these surveys is intended to be of use to members of the school as they work through the process of identifying priorities for special attention over the next several years.

All surveys asked respondents to rate statements concerning their school on a 5-point scale ranging from 1 (*strongly disagree*) to 5 (*strongly agree*). A sixth option, NA or not applicable, was available for those who thought the question did not apply to them. For this report all responses were recoded so that a rating of +2 (originally 5 on the scale) represents strongest agreement with the statement whereas a rating of −2 (originally 1) represents strongest *disagreement*. Ratings approaching 0 indicate weak agreement/disagreement or possible indifference.

This report presents the results of the surveys in three sections:

Section 1: This section provides results about teachers' perceptions of the current status of 10 characteristics of schools. Mean ratings of teachers in this school are compared with mean ratings of all elementary schools in the district. Not too much should be made of this comparison since schools face very different challenges and may be pursuing quite different priorities.

Figure 1 reports mean ratings of teachers' perceptions of the following characteristics:

- Mission and Goals
- Culture
- Core Tasks: Leadership
- Core Tasks: Management
- Core Tasks: Planning

- Core Tasks: Instructional Services
- Structure and Organization
- Information Collection and Decision Making
- Policies and Procedures
- Community Partnerships

Ratings of the ten characteristics of schools are reported in more detail on Figures 2 to 11. The horizontal axis on each chart identifies more specific components of each school characteristic and reports mean ratings of these components by teachers in your school and by teachers in all elementary schools in the district.

Section 2: This section reports all teachers' responses to individual items in the survey about the school. The first page in this section links individual survey items to the specific components reported in the Section 1 charts. The following pages provide three types of data for each item: the *number of teachers* who selected a response on the 5-point scale; teachers' *average or mean rating* of the item recoded on the −2 to +2 scale; and the *standard deviation*, which measures the spread of teacher ratings. The more teachers disagree with each other, which is reflected in responses spread across a wider range of the five response options, the larger the standard deviation. Neither NA responses nor blanks were included in calculating the item mean.

Section 3: This section reports students' responses to their survey. The bar graph at the beginning of the section summarizes student responses concerning their participation and identification with school as well as several other related matters (quality of instruction, family educational culture, perceptions of academic efficacy). Mean or averages responses are displayed separately for elementary, junior high, and high schools on Figure 12.

This section also reports all students' responses to individual items in their survey. The student report contains the same type of information that is provided for teachers in the previous section: *number of students responding, mean ratings, and standard deviation.*

The report has been designed to give you a broad overview of results first and then permit you to look in more detail at the information which you judge warrants the most urgent attention. Thus Section 1 begins with the broad school characteristics (Figure 1) rated by teachers, followed by components within each characteristic (Figures 2 to 11). Section 2 reports individual item results from which the components and characteristics are developed. Section 3 reports student results for five categories (Figure 12) and individual items.

Section 1: School Characteristics

In the form of bar graphs, this section provides the results of the surveys about teachers' perceptions of the current status of ten characteristics of your school. On each figure, the darker bar displays your school's ratings and the lighter bar displays the ratings of teachers in all elementary schools in your district.

Figure 1 reports mean ratings of teachers' perceptions of the following characteristics:

- Mission and Goals
- Culture
- Core Tasks: Leadership
- Core Tasks: Management
- Core Tasks: Planning
- Core Tasks: Instructional Services
- Structure and Organization
- Information Collection and Decision Making
- Policies and Procedures
- Community Partnerships

Figures 2 to 11 display the ratings of the 10 characteristics of school in more detail. The horizontal axis on each chart identifies specific components of the school characteristic and reports teachers' mean ratings of these components separately for your school and all elmentary schools in your district.

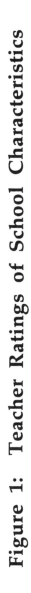

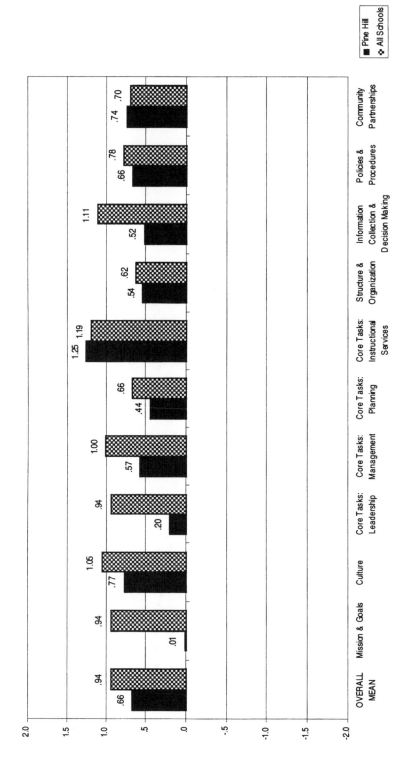

Figure 1: Teacher Ratings of School Characteristics

Scale: - 2 = Strongly Disagree to + 2 = Strongly Agree

Figure 4: Teacher Ratings of Core Tasks: Leadership

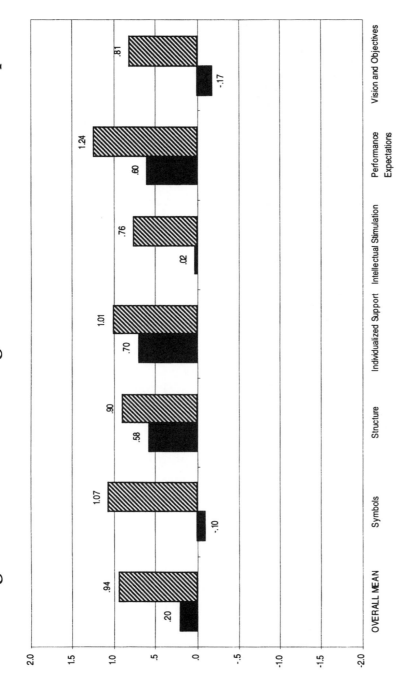

Scale: - 2 = Srongly Disagree to + 2 Strongly Agree

Figure 7: Teacher Ratings of Core Tasks: Instructional Services

Pine Hill
All Schools

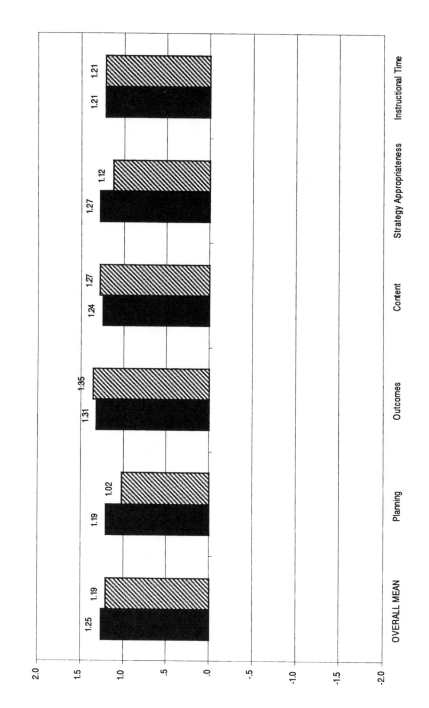

Scale: - 2 = Strongly Disagree to + 2 = Strongly Agree

Section 2: Teacher Responses to Individual Questionnaire Items

This section reports all teachers' responses to individual items in the survey. As noted in the Overview, the survey asked teachers to rate statements concerning their school on a 5-point scale ranging from 1 (*strongly disagree*) to 5 (*strongly agree*). A sixth option, NA or not applicable, was available for those who thought the question did not apply to them. For this report all responses were recoded so that a rating of +2 (originally 5 on the scale) represents strongest agreement with the statement whereas a rating of –2 represents strongest *disagreement*. Ratings approaching 0 indicate weak agreement/disagreement or possible indifference.

The next page in this section links the specific components shown on Figures 2 to 11 in Section 1 with the individual statements rated by teachers. The bar title from the figure is followed by the question numbers for the statements that measured the component.

Three types of data are provided for each item: the *number of teachers* who selected a response on the five-point scale; teachers' *average or mean rating* of the item recoded on the –2 to +2 scale; and the *standard deviation*, which measures the spread of teacher ratings. The more teachers disagree with each other, which is reflected in responses spread across a wider range of the five response options, the larger the standard deviation. Neither NA responses nor blanks were included in calculating the item mean.

These individual item results are organized in the same order as the characteristics and more specific components of the school were displayed in Section 1.

Survey Questions Measuring Specific Components of School Characteristics

	Question #		Question #		Question #
Mission and Goals					
1. Clarity	1-4	4. Use	13-18	6. Congruence	23-24
2. Meaningfulness	5-7	5. Timeliness	19-22	7. Basic Values	25-30
3. Awareness	8-12				
Culture					
1. Strength	1-5	3. Safety & Security	11-19	5. Professional Environment	27-32
2. Form	6-10	4. Student Focus	20-26		
Core Tasks: Leadership					
1. Symbolizing Professionalism	1-6	3. Providing Individualized Support	13-16	5. Holding Performance Expectations	24-26
2. Developing Collaborative Structures	7-12	4. Providing Intellectual Stimulation	17-23	6. Fostering Vision & Objectives	27-32
Core Tasks: Management					
1. Effective Staffing	1-6	3. Monitors School Activities	12-16	4. Community Focus	17-20
2. Instructional Support	7-11				
Core Tasks: Planning					
1. Relevant Information	1-3	4. Support & Understanding	15-22	6. Monitoring Goal Achievement	28-31
2. Systematic Review of Current Plan	4-9	5. Use of School Objectives	23-27	7. Monitoring Planning	32-34
3. Sources of School Objectives	10-14				
Core Tasks: Instructional Services					
1. Instructional Planning	1-5	3. Instructional Content	10-13	5. Instructional Time	19-24
2. Outcomes	6-9	4. Strategy Appropriateness	14-18		
Structure and Organization					
1. Instructional Time	1-4	3. Facilitating Professional Growth	8-12	5. Allocating Student Groupings	21-26
2. Working Conditions	5-7	4. Appropriate Structures	13-20		
Information Collection and Decision Making					
1. Systematic Collection	1-3	3. Openness to External Sources	9-12	4. Student Assessment Practices	13-21
2. Decentralized Decision Making	4-8			5. Uses of Assessment Information	22-26
Policies and Procedures					
1. Coherence	1-5	4. Special Needs Focus	16-23	7. Staff Development	34-40
2. Student Orientation	6-9	5. Student Counseling & Support	24-29	8. Resource Allocation	41-45
3. Student Awareness	10-15	6. Professional Focus	30-33		
Community Partnerships					
1. School-Community Cooperation	1-7	2. Parent-School Collaboration	8-19	3. Community Support Services	20-25

Example

TEACHER RATINGS OF SCHOOL CHARACTERISTICS:
Number of Respondents, Mean, and Standard Deviation

	N	Mean	SD
Core Tasks: School Leadership	**20**	**.20**	**.99**
Symbolizing Professionalism	**20**	**-.10**	**1.13**
1. Shows respect for staff by treating us as professionals.	20	.31	1.34
2. Sets a respectful tone for interaction with students.	20	.09	1.29
3. Demonstrates a willingness to change own practices in light of new understandings.	20	-.30	.95
4. Models problem-solving techniques that I can readily adapt for my work.	20	-.20	1.32
5. Promotes an atmosphere of caring and trust among staff.	20	-.31	1.25
6. Symbolizes success and accomplishment within our profession.	20	-.22	1.14
Developing Collaborative Structures	**20**	**.58**	**.98**
7. Delegates leadership for activities critical for achieving school goals.	20	.80	1.14
8. Distributes leadership broadly among the staff.	20	.59	.97
9. Ensures that we have adequate involvement in decision making.	20	.71	1.16
10. Supports an effective committee structure for decision making.	20	.49	1.08
11. Facilitates effective communication among staff.	20	.01	1.05
12. Provides an appropriate level of autonomy for us in our own decision making.	20	.92	1.10
32.			
Core Tasks: Instructional Services	**17**	**1.25**	**.24**
Instructional Planning	**17**	**1.19**	**.56**
1. My instruction is carefully planned to provide diverse activities and experiences.	17	1.25	.53
2. Our school's curriculum is clearly written and well understood by staff.	16	1.00	1.26
3. Teachers work together to avoid unnecessary redundancies.	16	.67	1.37
4. Our programs help students understand how a particular topic relates to their relevant prior knowledge.	17	.71	.95
5. I always establish a clear framework for instructional themes or activities.	17	1.86	.39
Outcomes	**17**	**1.31**	**.41**
6. Instructional practices are modified to support attainment of board learning outcomes.	17	.86	.38
7. My instructional goals, content, and student assessment practices are aligned.	17	1.43	.53
8. My instructional goals are compatible with the board learning outcomes.	17	1.29	.76
9. I help my students develop a clear understanding of the purposes for instruction.	17	1.71	.49
24.			

Scale: −2 = Strongly Disagree to +2 = Strongly Agree

Chapter 11

Using School and District Monitoring Information

Those aspects of the monitoring system described so far have concerned what information to collect and why. We have also alluded to Appendixes A and B, which contain survey instruments to assist in such information collection. This chapter provides guidelines for increasing the chances of schools and districts actually using and learning from monitoring-system information. As Madaus and Tan (1993) said in their reference to student test data, "It is not the form of the tests . . . that is important in determining the impact of a testing program on students, teachers, and schools. Instead, it is the use to which the results are put" (p. 73). The same can be said for monitoring-system information as well. Its use will determine the extent to which the monitoring system truly does make schools and districts smarter.

A depressingly large amount of evidence suggests that the results of formal evaluations are more often ignored than used. This is a waste of both resources and opportunity. In this concluding chapter, we worry about how results of applying the monitoring system can avoid this ignominious fate. The outcome of that worry is a set of guidelines intended to be helpful for those implementing the monitoring system in their own schools and districts. As a warm up to the guidelines, we clarify what it means to *use* the results of a formal monitoring process and examine some of the factors effecting such use. A general approach to fostering use of monitoring system results is briefly described along with a set of related guidelines.

THE MEANINGS OF "USE"

Let's suppose that, in one way or another, a district implements some locally appropriate version of the monitoring system next year and results appear in a report. Among those who receive the report are four secondary school principals in your district—Shalonda, Gerald, Reyhan, and Roberto. Shalonda is in the midst of a school accreditation process, sponsored by the state/province, involving considerable collection of data about her own school. She is having trouble just keeping on top of all the information being churned out of the accreditation process. This is information she assumes will meet her needs more directly than anything the district could possibly provide. Accordingly, she opts to file the report and read it "later."

In contrast to Shalonda, Gerald has a problem for which he has little helpful information: The school's retention rates have fallen significantly for the past 3 years. Gerald eagerly scans the district monitoring report to see if there is anything that might shed light on his problem. Seeing nothing about causes of dropout, he puts it aside, disappointed that it is not more relevant for him.

Reyhan's circumstances are similar to Gerald's: an obvious problem and no ready solution. The problem for Reyhan is the reticence of her senior-grade teachers to seriously consider what the new Senior Division Program might mean for them and to begin some planning for its implementation. As she reads the report, she begins to understand a bit better why the competitive culture she has fostered among department heads in her school may be having an effect opposite to what she intended. Reyhan assumed such competition would be a spur toward innovation, but she now suspects that it may be reducing risk-taking behavior and discouraging the serious consideration of district-initiated restructuring efforts. The monitoring report doesn't tell her what to do, but at least Reyhan thinks the problem has become clearer to her.

Roberto's response to the district monitoring report is unlike any of his three principal colleagues and quite straightforward. After Roberto introduced the report to his school improvement team, they saw in three of its recommendations for schools some courses of action that were well suited to their circumstances. Roberto and the team shared these recommendations with staff as a whole, and there was quick consensus that they should be implemented.

We see in the responses of these four principals the range of meanings of *use* applied to monitoring results. Shalonda provided a good example of *non-use*; she didn't even read the report. Gerald "used" the report only in the sense that he read portions of it—*some of the information was processed*—but then gave it no further thought. The uses of monitoring results for purposes of enlightenment or *conceptual understanding* are illustrated in Reyhan's response; this is considered use even though Reyhan's actions are not influenced, at least in the short term. Finally, *instrumental use* best describes how Roberto and his staff responded to the report; there was an obvious and direct connection between the monitoring report and their decisions and actions.

In none of these examples does one see *centralized*, instrumental use of monitoring system information as might be expected in a highly bureaucratized district (to recall some ground covered in Chapter 2). One does see *individual* enlightenment or con-ceptual understanding in Reyhan's responses to the results, a use associated in Chapter 2 with a community perspective on districts and schools. Roberto provides an example of how monitoring system results could be used in a learning organization—that is, by groups as well as by individuals. Of course, it would also count as organizational learning if Roberto's colleagues derived some greater collective understanding of their problems from the monitoring results without acting on the results as directly and instrumentally as they did.

EXPLAINING VARIATIONS IN USE OF MONITORING SYSTEM RESULTS

The different responses of Shalonda, Gerald, Reyhan, and Roberto illustrate not only the different types of use likely to be made of monitoring system results but also some of the reasons for such variation. Shalonda's non-use was due to the competing information provided by her school's ongoing accreditation process. Gerald's "processing-only" form of use was based on a quick judgment that the report was not *relevant* to his retention problem. Reyhan found the report especially timely because she was in the midst of puzzling over a problem of staff reticence on which the report shed some light. The content of the report was a big part of the reason for the ready use made of the report by Roberto and his staff: it was quite congruent with their own knowledge and offered directions that were immediately valued.

Ferreting out reasons such as these has been the goal of considerable research over the past 20 years. A relatively comprehensive set of these reasons (and relationships among them) has been identified in recent syntheses of this research (Cousins & Leithwood, 1986, 1993). Figure 11.1, displaying these results, identifies three broad categories of reasons: (a) reasons related to the monitoring system information or report of results itself; (b) reasons that depend on the district or school context in which results are to be used; and (c) reasons that arise from the interaction of people in the schools or districts responding to these activities and results.

With respect to monitoring system activities and results, evidence suggests that some form of productive use is more likely when

- monitoring activities are sophisticated and rigorous;
- those involved in conducting the monitoring are considered credible by the potential users of the monitoring information;
- the information is considered relevant to problems being addressed by the organization (recall Gerald's perfunctory use on these grounds);
- monitoring results are communicated in a clear, concise, and readily comprehendable form;
- findings are consistent with the way of thinking or the expectations of users (a likely reason for Roberto's response);
- results are made available in a timely fashion (giving rise, in part, to Reyhan's use of the results);
- the development and implementation of the monitoring process is collaborative and involves all stakeholders (participatory).

Whether or not these qualities associated with monitoring activities and results stimulate productive use depends on the context in which they are to be used—selected characteristics of the school or district and their staffs. Evidence suggests that use is more likely when

- potential users perceive a gap in their knowledge which monitoring system results can help fill (perhaps a second reason for Martha's use of the report was to improve her understanding of staff reticence);
- the focus of the monitoring system results is consistent with the focus of district or school improvement efforts;
- the "political climate" or priorities established by the school or district are consistent with directions proposed by the monitoring results;
- there is no other source of relevant information seriously competing for the attention of users (reminding us of why Eileen just set the monitoring report aside, unread);
- potential users have had previous positive experiences in making use of monitoring system-like evidence;
- potential users are open to new ideas and committed to improving their practices with assistance from whatever sources may be helpful.

As Figure 11.1 also indicates, amounts and types of use made of monitoring system results also depend on a third category of reasons, a category which we label *interactive processes*. This category of reasons suggests that use of results is fostered when

FIGURE 11.1. Factors Explaining Variations in the Use People Make of Monitoring System Results

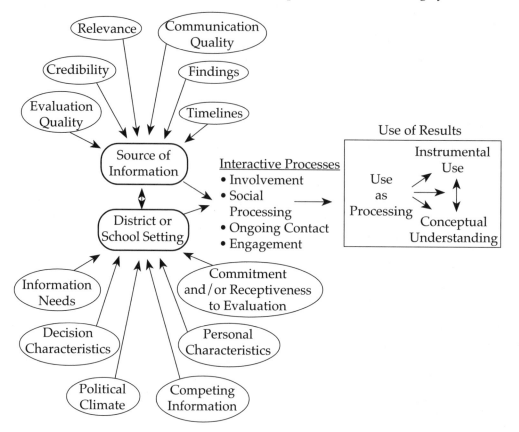

NOTE: Adapted from "Enhancing Knowledge Utilization as a Strategy for School Improvement," by B. Cousins and K. Leithwood, 1993, *Knowledge: Creation, Diffusion, Utilization, 14*(3), p. 308.

- school or district staffs have ample opportunities to consider the meaning of monitoring system results together (social processing);
- suitably extensive discussions occur among people so that they arrive at a deeper understanding of monitoring results and implications for their work (a version of this may have taken place in Roberto's school);
- people are engaged in communicating monitoring system activities and results to others; such engagement (as when teaching others) stimulates a level of understanding often not otherwise arrived at;
- people are involved not just at the stage of receiving and acting on monitoring system results but also in many of the monitoring system activities leading to the results;
- people have ongoing contact with others who might be of assistance in interpreting results, figuring out what changes in practice might be warranted and learning how to implement these practices.

So, we know quite a bit about why the results of monitoring system initiatives might sometimes be ignored, sometimes be only briefly and selectively sampled, and occasionally be acted on quite directly. In the following and final section of this chapter, we offer guidelines for encouraging use arising from both the framework and our experience in assisting people with the monitoring system.

The central question addressed in this final section of the book is: How can the monitoring system be implemented so that organizational learning occurs given a participatory approach to monitoring, and what is known about reasons why monitoring results are not used?

Since writing the first edition of this book, we have had opportunities to help many districts and schools use the monitoring system. In addition, one of our doctoral students (Ross Elliott) has recently completed a formal, in-depth, case study of monitoring system use in one large district, and in three schools in that district. Between our own experience and Elliott's case study data, we offer five quite practical pieces of advice about using the monitoring system to best effect. This advice is generally consistent, of course, with the broader literature on the use of monitoring systems summarized above.

Our own experience at the district level suggests that, as in many other matters involving school change, principals are absolutely crucial candidates for such education. Our experience also suggests that, within any group of principals, there will be enormous differences in their understandings about the importance of what the monitoring system measures and how the monitoring data might be directly useful for school improvement planning. There is also considerable difference among principals in their grasp of the simple statistics most likely to be used to summarize data. Not everyone knows the purposes and practical applications of such things as standard deviations.

At the school level, it is important to appreciate the classroom perspective of teachers; many of whom may not think explicitly about the school's culture and structures, for example, or immediately agree that data about such elements would be valuable. It is usually up to principals to provide teachers with opportunities to think about school-wide matters and their consequences for classroom instruction.

CONCLUSION: GUIDELINES FOR FOSTERING USE OF MONITORING SYSTEM INFORMATION

Guideline 1: Educating Participants About the Monitoring System

Guideline 2: Choose Credible Participants

As Figure 11.1 indicates, the credibility of those people associated with the monitoring system and its implementation are also an important influence on peoples' willingness to make use of the information it generates. Perceptions of credibility may not have much to do with the *technical* skills people bring to the monitoring process. Rather, and probably more important, credibility is more likely a function of those people being viewed as sensible, reasonable people who understand the context in which their colleagues are working and have demonstrated some form of leadership with their colleagues in the past. They ought to be "opinion leaders."

In one of Elliott's case schools, the principal and staff decided that they needed an external person to help them interpret and use their monitoring data. The person they selected turned out to be enormously helpful to the staff, in part because he was well known, respected, and trusted by staff from earlier associations with the school.

In this same school, the principal was predisposed to consider the monitoring data especially carefully because of his respect for the superintendent who had been involved in the district's decision to use the monitoring system originally, and his continuing interest in its use.

Guideline 3: Provide Tangible and Symbolic Support for the Process

This guideline acknowledges a number of important difficulties that require tangible attention if the monitoring is to be implemented successfully. Participation takes time. In particular, it competes with the time people have to devote to many other responsibilities. Implementing school or district monitoring means that scarce resources need to be redeployed in support of this effort. Because participation in monitoring offers substantial opportunities for new learning, one obvious source of resources (both time and money) for redeployment are resources currently being used for professional development activities.

Teachers, for example, often find that providing data for the monitoring system is quite enlightening. Finding time to fill out "yet another survey" often precedes the desired enlightenment. Sometimes, the care with which such data are provided, and the number of people who provide it, can be significantly enhanced by capturing 30 or 40 minutes at a staff meeting for the purpose.

Symbolic and psychological supports for participation in monitoring should be evident as well. For example, districts that reinforce the importance of making decisions based on good quality data provide symbolic support (and more) for peoples' participation in well-designed monitoring activities. Furthermore, schools and districts should ensure through their communication and publication processes that when decisions are made resulting from the monitoring information, all stakeholders are made aware of such action.

One district that has used the monitoring system collected district-level as well as school-level data. Central office staff then examined the district-level data carefully and announced to the schools changes in their own central office practices that they had made in response. This proved to be an important, symbolic gesture for fostering greater use of monitoring system data in many schools.

Participation takes time. In particular, it competes with the time people have to devote to many other responsibilities.

When people, viewed as leaders in the school or district, also devote their own time to participating in the monitoring process, this carries important symbolic weight encouraging both participation in the process and use of the subsequent results.

Data about school leadership in one of Elliott's case schools proved to be quite disappointing to the principal. Rather than belittle or ignore it, however, he responded quite directly to it with significant changes in his leadership style, after discussions with staff. Teachers were impressed with his response and examined the remainder of their data very carefully. Over the course of a year the staff significantly restructured their school.

Perceptions about the timeliness and the relevance of monitoring system results, as well as how much priority is to be given those results, in comparison with competing information, will be influenced by the link between priorities established by districts and schools and the focus of monitoring system activities. The monitoring system should be, and be seen to be, in direct service of district and school priorities. The relevance of the monitoring system information creates a responsive "political" climate for its use and fosters greater engagement in the process since more is clearly at stake in ignoring those results than would be the case were this link not substantial.

Guideline 4: Ensure Coherence Between School and District Priorities and the Focus for Monitoring

One district that has made extensive use of the monitoring system, for example, implemented it initially because one of that district's strategic planning goals was to develop and implement procedures for increasing district and school accountability. The monitoring system was adopted as a means of accomplishing that goal.

Guideline 5: Do It Again   Initial use of the monitoring system provokes a wide range of responses, some quite dependent on local history. Within the same school, for example, our experience suggests that responses can range from "It's about time," "This is interesting," and "Wow! I didn't know that" to "What now?", "Another survey," "Will this be used against us?" or "We could better use the money spent on this for textbooks." Versions of these responses are not uncommon to change. Actually using the monitoring system and discovering its utility clarifies some important issues. Such use makes it clear, for example, that

- the monitoring data are only as good as the care taken in responding to the surveys;
- the views of many of one's colleagues were not as presumed;
- important aspects of the school may be highlighted that otherwise would not have come to attention;
- the concrete and tangible quality of the data offers some very practical tools for school improvement decision making;
- the conversations among staff about what needs to be done in the school has been taken to a much higher, and more productive, level.

With these understandings in place, the next time the monitoring system is used there will be a greater number of serious responses from more people, less time needed to make sense of the results, and a smoother process for moving to action. The data can also be compared with previous results and changes in outcomes.

Specific, relevant data such as the monitoring system produces is the most pertinent information any jurisdiction can acquire in helping it to change the basic ideas that ground day-to-day life in schools, as Bryk and Hermanson noted at the beginning of this book.

Appendix A:
The School Surveys

This section includes survey instruments for measuring the current status of individual schools within a district. The 10 surveys in this section are as follows:

- School Mission and Goals
- School Culture
- School Core Tasks (three instruments about different aspects of the core tasks)
- School Structure and Organization
- School Information Collection and Decision Making
- School Policies and Procedures
- School-Community Partnerships
- Student Participation and Engagement: Family Educational Culture

The first 9 of these instruments are quite brief and should require less than 15 minutes to complete. The final instrument, to be completed by students, typically requires about 20 minutes.

School Mission and Goals

Respondent Role:

☐ STUDENT
☐ TEACHER
☐ ADMINISTRATOR
☐ SUPPORT STAFF (Secretary, Custodian,
       School Assistant, etc.)
☐ PARENT
☐ TRUSTEE
☐ COMMUNITY MEMBER (other than parent)
☐ OTHER (specify)

INSTRUCTIONS TO RESPONDENTS:

The purpose of this survey is to obtain information about what you think of certain aspects of the school giving the survey. The information will be used in an effort to improve education for students. Therefore, please read the instructions carefully and answer each question as honestly as possible. You should be able to complete this survey in about 5 minutes. Your response to the questionnaire will be anonymous and will be combined with those of others to reveal patterns. Responses from your school will be combined with responses from other schools.

We are interested in the extent to which you agree or disagree with the following statements.

For each statement, select and check ONE of the following responses:

1	2	3	4	NA
strongly agree	agree	disagree	strongly disagree	not applicable/ don't know

	strongly agree			strongly disagree	
1.1 Clarity	1	2	3	4	NA
1. I easily understand our school's mission statement.	☐	☐	☐	☐	☐
2. The staff easily understand our school's mission statement.	☐	☐	☐	☐	☐
3. The students easily understand our school's mission statement.	☐	☐	☐	☐	☐
4. The local community at large easily understands our school's mission statement.	☐	☐	☐	☐	☐
5. I easily understand our school's goals.	☐	☐	☐	☐	☐
6. The staff easily understand our school's goals.	☐	☐	☐	☐	☐
7. The students easily understand our school's goals.	☐	☐	☐	☐	☐
8. The local community easily understands our school's goals.	☐	☐	☐	☐	☐

1.2 Meaningfulness

9. I am committed to the goals and mission of our school.	☐	☐	☐	☐	☐
10. My beliefs are reflected in our goals and mission statement.	☐	☐	☐	☐	☐
11. The staff are committed to the goals and mission of our school.	☐	☐	☐	☐	☐
12. Parents are committed to the goals and mission of our school.	☐	☐	☐	☐	☐
13. The beliefs of the community are reflected in the goals and mission statement.	☐	☐	☐	☐	☐
14. Our school's goals and mission are worth striving to achieve.	☐	☐	☐	☐	☐
15. Our school's goals and mission reflect the needs of the local community.	☐	☐	☐	☐	☐

1.3 Awareness

16. Staff in our school work toward the same goals. □ □ □ □ □
17. We work toward consensus in establishing priorities for our school's goals. □ □ □ □ □
18. Our school's goals are displayed prominently. □ □ □ □ □
19. Our mission statement is displayed prominently. □ □ □ □ □
20. My colleagues and I agree on the meaning of our school's mission statement. □ □ □ □ □
21. My colleagues and I agree on the intent of our school's goals. □ □ □ □ □

1.4 Use

22. Our school's goals are reflected in our school plans. □ □ □ □ □
23. Our school's goals are used to establish priorities in the school budget. □ □ □ □ □
24. Our discipline practices reflect our school's goals and mission. □ □ □ □ □
25. Our school's goals and mission are reflected in classroom practice. □ □ □ □ □
26. The parent group activities reflect our school's goals and mission. □ □ □ □ □
27. Our school's goals and mission influence curriculum and instruction in our school. □ □ □ □ □

1.5 Currency

28. We regularly evaluate our progress toward achievement of our school's goals. □ □ □ □ □
29. Our school's goals have been reviewed in the past year. □ □ □ □ □
30. The staff discuss our school's goals and mission when developing annual plans. □ □ □ □ □
31. Our school's goals and mission are reviewed as changes occur in the school demographics. □ □ □ □ □
32. Our school's mission statement has been revised in the past year. □ □ □ □ □

1.6 Congruence

33. Our school's goals agree with the district's goals. □ □ □ □ □
34. Our school's mission statement is compatible with the mission statement for the district. □ □ □ □ □

1.7 Immediate Focus

35. Teachers engage in problem solving to generate our school plans. □ □ □ □ □
36. The action of teachers supports our school's goals. □ □ □ □ □
37. The organization of our school facilitates achievement of our school's goals. □ □ □ □ □
38. Administrative practices support the attainment of our school's goals. □ □ □ □ □

1.8 Long-Range Focus

39. Our school's goals encourage a broad range of student achievement (beyond the intellectual-cognitive area). □ □ □ □ □
40. Our school's goals emphasize developing students' commitment to lifelong learning. □ □ □ □ □
41. Our school's goals emphasize developing citizenship. □ □ □ □ □
42. Our school's goals emphasize development of self-worth. □ □ □ □ □
43. Our school's goals are driven by the mission statement of our school. □ □ □ □ □
44. Our school's goals emphasize developing life skills. □ □ □ □ □

School Culture

Respondent Role:

☐ STUDENT
☐ TEACHER
☐ ADMINISTRATOR
☐ SUPPORT STAFF (Secretary, Custodian,
    School Assistant, etc.)
☐ PARENT
☐ TRUSTEE
☐ COMMUNITY MEMBER (other than parent)
☐ OTHER (specify)

INSTRUCTIONS TO RESPONDENTS:

The purpose of this survey is to obtain information about what you think of certain aspects of the school giving the survey. The information will be used in an effort to improve education for students. Therefore, please read the instructions carefully and answer each question as honestly as possible. You should be able to complete this survey in about 5 minutes. Your response to the questionnaire will be anonymous and will be combined with those of others to reveal patterns. Responses from your school will be combined with responses from other schools.

We are interested in the extent to which you agree or disagree with the following statements.
For each statement, select and check ONE of the following responses:

1	2	3	4	NA
strongly agree	agree	disagree	strongly disagree	not applicable/ don't know

2.1 Strength

	strongly agree 1	2	3	strongly disagree 4	NA
1. Most teachers in our school share a similar set of values, beliefs, and attitudes related to teaching and learning.	☐	☐	☐	☐	☐
2. I have close working relationships with my colleagues in our school.	☐	☐	☐	☐	☐
3. There is ongoing, collaborative work among teachers in our school/department.	☐	☐	☐	☐	☐
4. Our school administrators share teachers' values, beliefs, and attitudes related to teaching and learning.	☐	☐	☐	☐	☐
5. There is a strong, positive relationship between students and staff in our school.	☐	☐	☐	☐	☐
6. Our school celebrates the achievements of staff and students.	☐	☐	☐	☐	☐

2.2 Form

7. I have frequent conversations about teaching practices with colleagues in our school.	☐	☐	☐	☐	☐
8. I frequently work with colleague(s) in our school to prepare unit outlines and/or instructional materials.	☐	☐	☐	☐	☐
9. I share my professional expertise by demonstrating new teaching practices for colleagues.	☐	☐	☐	☐	☐
10. We observe each other teaching and then discuss our observations to gain better understanding of our own teaching strategies.	☐	☐	☐	☐	☐
11. I adhere to school curriculum decisions agreed on in collaboration with my colleagues.	☐	☐	☐	☐	☐

2.3.1 Content is safe and orderly

12. I usually work through problems with my students, rather than refer them to the administration. □ □ □ □ □
13. I feel safe in our school. □ □ □ □ □
14. Students feel safe in our school. □ □ □ □ □
15. Our school is virtually free of vandalism. □ □ □ □ □
16. Our school monitors student behavior. □ □ □ □ □
17. I feel comfortable interacting with the students in our school. □ □ □ □ □
18. Our school has relatively few discipline problems. □ □ □ □ □
19. Inappropriate student behavior is dealt with effectively in our school. □ □ □ □ □
20. The consequences for inappropriate behavior in our school are immediate and consistent. □ □ □ □ □

2.3.2 Content is positive

21. Our school emphasizes creating a positive atmosphere for our students. □ □ □ □ □
22. Our staff praise and reward students' exemplary efforts and behavior. □ □ □ □ □

2.3.3 Content is student centered

23. Students in our school need to meet or exceed clearly defined expectations. □ □ □ □ □
24. I meet with students informally outside school hours. □ □ □ □ □
25. I hold high expectations for individual student learning and behavior. □ □ □ □ □
26. I model lifelong learning for my students. □ □ □ □ □
27. Our school recognizes teachers who are exemplary in their classroom and schoolwide practices. □ □ □ □ □
28. Our school administration acts in the best interests of the individual students. □ □ □ □ □

2.3.4 Content fosters learning for students

29. Planning for and helping students learn is my most important work. □ □ □ □ □
30. My school administrators protect my classroom instructional time. □ □ □ □ □
31. My colleagues make effective use of classroom time. □ □ □ □ □

2.3.5 Content is designed to provide a professional work environment for staff

32. Strong, positive relationships between staff and school administration facilitate implementation of new programs. □ □ □ □ □
33. I frequently implement new programs or new teaching strategies. □ □ □ □ □
34. I engage in ongoing, professional development for myself. □ □ □ □ □
35. I am motivated to implement new programs. □ □ □ □ □
36. I am satisfied with my job. □ □ □ □ □
37. Administrators in my school encourage professional risk taking and experimentation. □ □ □ □ □
38. Administrators in my school adjust priorities to support professional risk taking and experimentation. □ □ □ □ □

School Core Tasks (a)

Respondent Role:

☐ STUDENT
☐ TEACHER
☐ ADMINISTRATOR
☐ SUPPORT STAFF (Secretary, Custodian, School Assistant, etc.)
☐ PARENT
☐ TRUSTEE
☐ COMMUNITY MEMBER (other than parent)
☐ OTHER (specify)

INSTRUCTIONS TO RESPONDENTS:

The purpose of this survey is to obtain information about what you think of certain aspects of the school giving the survey. The information will be used in an effort to improve education for students. Therefore, please read the instructions carefully and answer each question as honestly as possible. You should be able to complete this survey in about 5 minutes. Your response to the questionnaire will be anonymous and will be combined with those of others to reveal patterns. Responses from your school will be combined with responses from other schools.

We are interested in the extent to which you agree or disagree with the following statements.

For each statement, select and check ONE of the following responses:

1	2	3	4	NA
strongly agree	agree	disagree	strongly disagree	not applicable/ don't know

	strongly agree			strongly disagree	
3.1.1 School Planning—Captures relevant information	**1**	**2**	**3**	**4**	**NA**
1. I have opportunities to provide input into our school plan.	☐	☐	☐	☐	☐
2. Parents/community members are involved in developing our school plan.	☐	☐	☐	☐	☐
3. School planning is based on cooperative decision making.	☐	☐	☐	☐	☐
4. My professional needs are being met by our school plan.	☐	☐	☐	☐	☐
3.1.2 School Planning—Systematic review of current plan					
5. Our school plan is reviewed systematically.	☐	☐	☐	☐	☐
6. Our school plan is changed to meet the changing needs of students and the community.	☐	☐	☐	☐	☐
7. Review of our school plan is facilitated by the systematic collection of data on our school's strengths and areas requiring improvement.	☐	☐	☐	☐	☐
8. Our school plan encourages me to enhance the learning environment.	☐	☐	☐	☐	☐
9. Data on student achievement are used in reviewing our school plan.	☐	☐	☐	☐	☐
3.1.3 School Planning—Sources of school goals					
10. Our school goals reflect district beliefs and goals.	☐	☐	☐	☐	☐
11. Parental aspirations are sources of our school goals.	☐	☐	☐	☐	☐
12. Political priorities affect school goals.	☐	☐	☐	☐	☐
13. School goals reflect political realities.	☐	☐	☐	☐	☐
14. School planning is informed by relevant educational research.	☐	☐	☐	☐	☐

3.1.4 School Planning—Encourages support and understanding

15. I understand how our school plans are developed. □ □ □ □ □
16. I am encouraged to collaborate in our school planning process. □ □ □ □ □
17. I support the process used to develop our school plans. □ □ □ □ □
18. The outcomes of our planning process are very worthwhile. □ □ □ □ □
19. I understand the intended outcomes of our planning process. □ □ □ □ □
20. The stakeholder groups in our community support our school planning process. □ □ □ □ □
21. The stakeholder groups in our community support the outcomes of our school planning process. □ □ □ □ □
22. I am aware of our school planning processes. □ □ □ □ □

3.1.5 School Planning—Use of school goals

23. Discussion about school goals and the means of achieving them is a regular part of staff meetings and/or in-service sessions in our school. □ □ □ □ □
24. I use school goals as a primary source of direction in my work. □ □ □ □ □
25. I have sustained discussion of school goals with my colleagues. □ □ □ □ □
26. Our planning process results in school goals that are a useful guide for my work. □ □ □ □ □
27. I make decisions using our school plan. □ □ □ □ □

3.1.6 School Planning—Monitoring goal achievement

28. Our school has developed a process for monitoring achievement of school goals. □ □ □ □ □
29. Achievement of school goals is monitored in our school. □ □ □ □ □
30. Improvement in student achievement is the main criterion for determining progress in achieving school goals. □ □ □ □ □
31. The process of monitoring achievement of school goals is a learning opportunity for all involved. □ □ □ □ □
32. The student's role as learner is the focus of school planning. □ □ □ □ □

3.1.7 School Planning—Evaluation of planning

33. We monitor our school planning process to determine whether the process helps us achieve our school goals. □ □ □ □ □
34. Our school has developed a process for evaluating school planning. □ □ □ □ □
35. Our school has a process for monitoring the influence of school planning on outcomes. □ □ □ □ □

3.1.8 School Planning—Process outcomes

36. I am informed regularly of the outcomes of our school planning process. □ □ □ □ □
37. Outcomes of our school planning process are shared regularly with all stakeholders in our community. □ □ □ □ □

School Core Tasks (b)

Respondent Role:

☐ STUDENT
☐ TEACHER
☐ ADMINISTRATOR
☐ SUPPORT STAFF (Secretary, Custodian, School Assistant, etc.)
☐ PARENT
☐ TRUSTEE
☐ COMMUNITY MEMBER (other than parent)
☐ OTHER (specify)

INSTRUCTIONS TO RESPONDENTS:

The purpose of this survey is to obtain information about what you think of certain aspects of the school giving the survey. The information will be used in an effort to improve education for students. Therefore, please read the instructions carefully and answer each question as honestly as possible. You should be able to complete this survey in about 5 minutes. Your response to the questionnaire will be anonymous and will be combined with those of others to reveal patterns. Responses from your school will be combined with responses from other schools.

We are interested in the extent to which you agree or disagree with the following statements.

For each statement, select and check ONE of the following responses:

1	2	3	4	NA
strongly agree	agree	disagree	strongly disagree	not applicable/ don't know

	strongly agree			strongly disagree	
3.2.1 Instructional Services—Instructional planning	1	2	3	4	NA
1. My instruction is carefully planned to provide diverse activities and experiences for my students.	☐	☐	☐	☐	☐
2. Our school's curriculum is clearly written and well understood by staff.	☐	☐	☐	☐	☐
3. Ministry curriculum is collaboratively developed to meet our school's needs.	☐	☐	☐	☐	☐
4. Teachers work together to address potential redundancy.	☐	☐	☐	☐	☐
5. Our programs help students understand how a particular topic relates to their relevant prior knowledge.	☐	☐	☐	☐	☐
6. I always establish a clear framework for instructional themes or activities in my classroom.	☐	☐	☐	☐	☐

3.2.2 Instructional Services—Instructional goals

7. Instructional practices in our school are modified to be compatible with school goals and priorities.	☐	☐	☐	☐	☐
8. My instructional goals, content, and student assessment practices are aligned.	☐	☐	☐	☐	☐
9. My instructional goals are compatible with school, district, and state/ provincial goals and priorities.	☐	☐	☐	☐	☐
10. I help my students develop a clear understanding of the purposes for instruction.	☐	☐	☐	☐	☐

3.2.3 Instructional Services—Instructional content

11. Our school offers a strong academic curriculum.	☐	☐	☐	☐	☐
12. Our school provides opportunity for curriculum enrichment.	☐	☐	☐	☐	☐
13. Our school's curriculum challenges our students to exert their best effort.	☐	☐	☐	☐	☐
14. Our school provides a rigorous core curriculum for most of our students.	☐	☐	☐	☐	☐

3.2.4 Instructional Services—Instructional strategy appropriateness

15. Teachers in our school are becoming skilled in the use of a large repertoire of instructional strategies.	☐	☐	☐	☐	☐
16. Students are given opportunity to determine their learning activities.	☐	☐	☐	☐	☐
17. My instructional strategies enable students to construct their own knowledge.	☐	☐	☐	☐	☐
18. I take students' interests, needs, and experiences into account when planning learning opportunities.	☐	☐	☐	☐	☐
19. My classroom is a comfortable learning environment with minimal distraction from instructional purposes.	☐	☐	☐	☐	☐

3.2.5 Instructional Services—Instructional strategy use

20. My curriculum makes meaningful linkages between learning opportunities and our students' lives and experiences.	☐	☐	☐	☐	☐
21. My curriculum stresses learning skills and applications that connect with the world beyond the school.	☐	☐	☐	☐	☐

The following is a list of some instructional strategies; indicate the extent to which you use:

	frequently	occasionally	seldom	never
22. small group learning	☐	☐	☐	☐
23. cooperative group learning	☐	☐	☐	☐
24. individualized instruction	☐	☐	☐	☐
25. instruction to the whole class	☐	☐	☐	☐
26. instruction to small groups	☐	☐	☐	☐
27. peer tutoring	☐	☐	☐	☐
28. differentiated assignments	☐	☐	☐	☐
29. group projects	☐	☐	☐	☐
30. independent study	☐	☐	☐	☐

	strongly agree			strongly disagree	
	1	2	3	4	NA
31. I maintain a fairly rapid pace of instruction in my classes.	☐	☐	☐	☐	☐

3.2.6 Instructional Services—Instructional time

	1	2	3	4	NA
	☐	☐	☐	☐	☐
32. Time lost to student absenteeism and lateness is minimized.	☐	☐	☐	☐	☐
33. I always begin my classes promptly.	☐	☐	☐	☐	☐
34. I keep transition times to a minimum.	☐	☐	☐	☐	☐
35. I manage student behavior in a way that minimizes disruptions during class.	☐	☐	☐	☐	☐
36. Student time-on-task is consistently high in my classes.	☐	☐	☐	☐	☐

School Core Tasks (c)

Respondent Role:

☐ STUDENT
☐ TEACHER
☐ ADMINISTRATOR
☐ SUPPORT STAFF (Secretary, Custodian, School Assistant, etc.)
☐ PARENT
☐ TRUSTEE
☐ COMMUNITY MEMBER (other than parent)
☐ OTHER (specify)

INSTRUCTIONS TO RESPONDENTS:

The purpose of this survey is to obtain information about what you think of certain aspects of the school giving the survey. The information will be used in an effort to improve education for students. Therefore, please read the instructions carefully and answer each question as honestly as possible. You should be able to complete this survey in about 5 minutes. Your response to the questionnaire will be anonymous and will be combined with those of others to reveal patterns. Responses from your school will be combined with responses from other schools.

We are interested in the extent to which you agree or disagree with the following statements.
For each statement, select and check ONE of the following responses:

1	2	3	4	NA
strongly agree	agree	disagree	strongly disagree	not applicable/ don't know

	strongly agree			strongly disagree	
3.3.1 Management of School Operations—Staffing	1	2	3	4	NA
1. The teacher's expertise is of paramount importance in staffing.	☐	☐	☐	☐	☐
2. The process of staff recruitment is fair and equitable.	☐	☐	☐	☐	☐
3. Present staff welcome and value new staff members.	☐	☐	☐	☐	☐
4. The contributions of all staff members, new and established, are valued equally.	☐	☐	☐	☐	☐
5. Our school administrators involve present staff members in hiring new staff.	☐	☐	☐	☐	☐
6. Our staff recruitment policies recognize the importance of placing staff in areas of competence and expertise.	☐	☐	☐	☐	☐

3.3.2 Management of School Operations—Instructional support

7. Our school administrators provide organizational support for teacher interaction on a regular basis.	☐	☐	☐	☐	☐
8. Disruptions of instructional time are minimized.	☐	☐	☐	☐	☐
9. Resources and technical assistance are available to help staff improve effectiveness.	☐	☐	☐	☐	☐
10. The school administrators regularly observe classroom activities.	☐	☐	☐	☐	☐
11. After classroom observations, our administrators work with teachers to improve their effectiveness.	☐	☐	☐	☐	☐
12. The school administrators frequently participate in discussions of educational issues.	☐	☐	☐	☐	☐

3.3.3 Management of School Operations—Monitoring school activities

13. Our school administrators' presence is positive. □ □ □ □ □
14. Our school administrators are visible within the school. □ □ □ □ □
15. Our school administrators are easily accessible to students and staff. □ □ □ □ □
16. Our school administrators' interest in students' progress is evident in their actions. □ □ □ □ □
17. Our school administrators frequently review student progress. □ □ □ □ □

3.3.4 Management of School Operations—Decision-making processes

18. Decisions in our school are a product of a process that involves all relevant information. □ □ □ □ □
19. The information-gathering process that precedes a decision is nondiscriminatory, all-inclusive, and equitable. □ □ □ □ □
20. Our school's decision-making processes are adjustable to fit the circumstances of the particular issue under consideration. □ □ □ □ □

3.3.5 Management of School Operations—Community focus

21. Our school administrators are sensitive to the community's aspirations and requests. □ □ □ □ □
22. Our school administrators attempt to plan and work with community representatives. □ □ □ □ □
23. Our school administrators will seek to incorporate the characteristics and values of the community in the operation of the school. □ □ □ □ □
24. Our school administrators have established a productive working relationship with the community. □ □ □ □ □
25. Our school administrators have secured a high degree of autonomy for the school within the district. □ □ □ □ □

3.4.1 School Leadership—Provides vision and/or inspiration

Leadership in this school:
26. Has both the capacity and judgment to overcome most obstacles □ □ □ □ □
27. Excites us with visions of what we may be able to accomplish if we work together □ □ □ □ □
28. Makes us feel and act like leaders □ □ □ □ □
29. Gives us a sense of overall purpose for our work □ □ □ □ □
30. Encourages innovation/change in consultation with staff □ □ □ □ □

3.4.2 School Leadership—Models behavior

Leadership in this school:
31. Leads by "doing," rather than simply by "telling" □ □ □ □ □
32. Symbolizes success and accomplishment □ □ □ □ □
33. Demonstrates effective interpersonal skills □ □ □ □ □
34. Commands respect from most staff in our school □ □ □ □ □
35. Demonstrates exemplary pedagogical skills □ □ □ □ □
36. Participates actively in classroom instruction □ □ □ □ □
37. Demonstrates consistent behaviors and attitudes when interacting with staff and students □ □ □ □ □

3.4.3 School Leadership—Provides individualized support

Leadership in this school:

38. Provides the necessary resources to support my implementation of new programs ☐ ☐ ☐ ☐ ☐
39. Treats me as an individual with unique needs and expertise ☐ ☐ ☐ ☐ ☐
40. Consults me when initiating actions that affect my work ☐ ☐ ☐ ☐ ☐
41. Responds to my personal and professional concerns with consideration ☐ ☐ ☐ ☐ ☐

3.4.4 School Leadership—Provides intellectual stimulation

Leadership in this school:

42. Challenges me to reexamine some basic assumptions I have about my work ☐ ☐ ☐ ☐ ☐
43. Stimulates me to think about what I am doing for my students ☐ ☐ ☐ ☐ ☐
44. Provides information that helps me think of ways to implement new programs ☐ ☐ ☐ ☐ ☐
45. Provides for extended training to develop my knowledge and skills ☐ ☐ ☐ ☐ ☐
46. Provides me with information on current educational thought on a variety of issues ☐ ☐ ☐ ☐ ☐

3.4.5 School Leadership—Fosters commitment to group goals

Leadership in this school:

47. Provides for our participation in the process of developing school goals ☐ ☐ ☐ ☐ ☐
48. Encourages teachers to work toward the same goals ☐ ☐ ☐ ☐ ☐
49. Uses the consultative approach with staff to generate school goals ☐ ☐ ☐ ☐ ☐
50. Works toward whole staff consensus in establishing priorities for school goals ☐ ☐ ☐ ☐ ☐
51. Encourages us regularly to evaluate our progress toward achievement of school goals ☐ ☐ ☐ ☐ ☐

3.4.6 School Leadership—Encourages high performance

Leadership in this school:

52. Has high expectations for us as professionals ☐ ☐ ☐ ☐ ☐
53. Encourages high performance from us ☐ ☐ ☐ ☐ ☐
54. Informs us of what high performance means ☐ ☐ ☐ ☐ ☐
55. Helps us feel and act like leaders ☐ ☐ ☐ ☐ ☐

3.4.7 School Leadership—Provides contingent reward

Leadership in this school:

56. Frequently acknowledges our performance ☐ ☐ ☐ ☐ ☐
57. Pays us personal compliments for our work ☐ ☐ ☐ ☐ ☐
58. Provides recognition for special work ☐ ☐ ☐ ☐ ☐
59. Helps us get those resources we decide we want ☐ ☐ ☐ ☐ ☐
60. Uses a reward system for professional improvement ☐ ☐ ☐ ☐ ☐

3.4.8 School Leadership—Encourages individual improvement

Leadership in this school:

61. Enhances my professional growth by sharing leadership responsibility with me ☐ ☐ ☐ ☐ ☐
62. Encourages me to take initiative in my work ☐ ☐ ☐ ☐ ☐
63. Encourages me always to improve my performance ☐ ☐ ☐ ☐ ☐

School Structure and Organization

Respondent Role:

- ☐ STUDENT
- ☐ TEACHER
- ☐ ADMINISTRATOR
- ☐ SUPPORT STAFF (Secretary, Custodian, School Assistant, etc.)
- ☐ PARENT
- ☐ TRUSTEE
- ☐ COMMUNITY MEMBER (other than parent)
- ☐ OTHER (specify)

INSTRUCTIONS TO RESPONDENTS:

The purpose of this survey is to obtain information about what you think of certain aspects of the school giving the survey. The information will be used in an effort to improve education for students. Therefore, please read the instructions carefully and answer each question as honestly as possible. You should be able to complete this survey in about 5 minutes. Your response to the questionnaire will be anonymous and will be combined with those of others to reveal patterns. Responses from your school will be combined with responses from other schools.

We are interested in the extent to which you agree or disagree with the following statements.

For each statement, select and check ONE of the following responses:

1	2	3	4	NA
strongly agree	agree	disagree	strongly disagree	not applicable/ don't know

	strongly agree			strongly disagree	
4.1 Instructional Time	1	2	3	4	NA
1. Our school meets all legal requirements regarding instructional time, to my knowledge.	☐	☐	☐	☐	☐
2. Our school meets all contractual requirements regarding instructional time, to my knowledge.	☐	☐	☐	☐	☐
3. Our school day is structured for maximum instructional use.	☐	☐	☐	☐	☐
4. Our school day is structured for minimum noninstructional use.	☐	☐	☐	☐	☐
5. Our school year is structured to maximize instructional time.	☐	☐	☐	☐	☐
6. Our school year is structured to minimize noninstructional time.	☐	☐	☐	☐	☐
4.2 Working Conditions					
7. Student timetables provide for extended blocks of time.	☐	☐	☐	☐	☐
8. Our timetable is organized to make provision for collaborative planning time.	☐	☐	☐	☐	☐
9. The organization of our school (e.g., timetable) facilitates flexible classroom-level decision making within the day.	☐	☐	☐	☐	☐
10. Teachers in our school have access to adequate clerical support.	☐	☐	☐	☐	☐

4.3 Facilitating Professional Growth

11. Collaboration among staff is encouraged by our school's organizational structure. ☐ ☐ ☐ ☐ ☐
12. Our school provides opportunities for collaboration with colleagues outside the school. ☐ ☐ ☐ ☐ ☐
13. Our school has effective procedures for making new ideas from external sources easily accessible for staff. ☐ ☐ ☐ ☐ ☐
14. Our school provides workshops that help make new ideas meaningful. ☐ ☐ ☐ ☐ ☐
15. Our school makes time for us to study documents that assist in making new ideas meaningful. ☐ ☐ ☐ ☐ ☐

4.4 Maximizing Student Learning

16. We work in teams in which several teachers assume responsibility for the same group of students. ☐ ☐ ☐ ☐ ☐
17. The structures of our school support teacher collaboration to maximize student learning opportunities. ☐ ☐ ☐ ☐ ☐
18. The structures of our school support teacher initiative to maximize student learning opportunities. ☐ ☐ ☐ ☐ ☐
19. The structures of our school support teacher leadership to maximize student learning opportunities. ☐ ☐ ☐ ☐ ☐
20. The structures of our school support teacher risk taking to maximize student learning opportunities. ☐ ☐ ☐ ☐ ☐

4.5 Allocation of Student Groupings

21. Assignment of students to classes is based primarily on student needs (rather than on teacher or administrator preferences). ☐ ☐ ☐ ☐ ☐
22. Assignment of students to classes is based on student-teacher ratio. ☐ ☐ ☐ ☐ ☐
23. Students work in heterogeneous groups within their classes. ☐ ☐ ☐ ☐ ☐
24. Flexible groupings, based on different criteria (e.g., multiage, ability, interest) are used for instructional purposes. ☐ ☐ ☐ ☐ ☐
25. Criteria used to allocate students to a grouping focus on their needs. ☐ ☐ ☐ ☐ ☐
26. Criteria used to allocate students to a grouping focus on my instructional purposes. ☐ ☐ ☐ ☐ ☐
27. Gifted students work in homogeneous ability groupings in one or two areas of especially high aptitude or interest. ☐ ☐ ☐ ☐ ☐
28. Procedures for allocating students to homogeneous groups provide for review of allocation decisions and reallocation. ☐ ☐ ☐ ☐ ☐

School Information Collection and Decision Making

Respondent Role:

☐ STUDENT

☐ TEACHER

☐ ADMINISTRATOR

☐ SUPPORT STAFF (Secretary, Custodian, School Assistant, etc.)

☐ PARENT

☐ TRUSTEE

☐ COMMUNITY MEMBER (other than parent)

☐ OTHER (specify)

INSTRUCTIONS TO RESPONDENTS:

The purpose of this survey is to obtain information about what you think of certain aspects of the school giving the survey. The information will be used in an effort to improve education for students. Therefore, please read the instructions carefully and answer each question as honestly as possible. You should be able to complete this survey in about 5 minutes. Your response to the questionnaire will be anonymous and will be combined with those of others to reveal patterns. Responses from your school will be combined with responses from other schools.

We are interested in the extent to which you agree or disagree with the following statements.

For each statement, select and check ONE of the following responses:

1	2	3	4	NA
strongly agree	agree	disagree	strongly disagree	not applicable/ don't know

	strongly agree			strongly disagree	
5.1 Systematic Collection	1	2	3	4	NA
1. In our school, a variety of types of data (e.g., marks, attendance, work habits, counselor reports, LA assessments) about individual student progress is collected regularly.	☐	☐	☐	☐	☐
2. In our school, teacher performance is monitored through regular reviews by a school administrator.	☐	☐	☐	☐	☐
3. In our school, teacher performance is monitored through regular peer review.	☐	☐	☐	☐	☐
4. In our school, teacher performance is regularly monitored through such means as government exam results, student pass/fail rates, and attendance/ dropout rates.	☐	☐	☐	☐	☐
5.2 Decentralized Decision Making					
5. In our school, teachers have the opportunity to participate in most significant school-level policy decisions.	☐	☐	☐	☐	☐
6. In my classroom, I have considerable autonomy in making decisions about implementing curriculum.	☐	☐	☐	☐	☐
7. In my classroom, I have considerable flexibility in deciding on instructional practices.	☐	☐	☐	☐	☐

5.3 School Improvement Decisions

8. In our school, decision making for school improvement initiatives is shared with teachers.   ☐ ☐ ☐ ☐ ☐

9. I take responsibility for solving most of the problems I encounter during school improvement initiatives.   ☐ ☐ ☐ ☐ ☐

10. Our school has a steering committee to manage the change process.   ☐ ☐ ☐ ☐ ☐

5.4 Openness to External Sources

11. Our staff is open to assistance from experts external to the school when we think it is necessary.   ☐ ☐ ☐ ☐ ☐

12. Our staff is open to new ideas and teaching methods from external sources.   ☐ ☐ ☐ ☐ ☐

13. Our school uses external expertise for support in solving problems.   ☐ ☐ ☐ ☐ ☐

14. Our school brings in external expertise for staff development.   ☐ ☐ ☐ ☐ ☐

5.5 Student Assessment Practices

15. Teachers in this school use a wide variety of assessment methods to provide authentic assessment of student achievement.   ☐ ☐ ☐ ☐ ☐

16. We are developing a good match between our assessment strategies and our curriculum objectives.   ☐ ☐ ☐ ☐ ☐

Our assessment practices include: ☐ ☐ ☐ ☐ ☐

17. Observing student products, performances, and learning processes   ☐ ☐ ☐ ☐ ☐

18. Collaboration with students to compile portfolios of samples of their work   ☐ ☐ ☐ ☐ ☐

Our evaluation practices include: ☐ ☐ ☐ ☐ ☐

19. Comparing students' current and past products, performances, and processes for learning   ☐ ☐ ☐ ☐ ☐

20. Comparing students to a wide range of developmental tendencies and expectations   ☐ ☐ ☐ ☐ ☐

21. Student reflection and self-evaluation processes to interpret their own learning   ☐ ☐ ☐ ☐ ☐

22. My colleagues and I agree about criteria for student assessment, evaluation, and reporting.   ☐ ☐ ☐ ☐ ☐

23. Our assessment, evaluation, and reporting practices reflect the learning opportunities provided.   ☐ ☐ ☐ ☐ ☐

5.6 Student Assessment Information

24. Assessment information is used to plan further learning opportunities for individuals and groups.   ☐ ☐ ☐ ☐ ☐

25. Our assessment practices include discussions and conferences with students.   ☐ ☐ ☐ ☐ ☐

26. We use the results of student evaluation to plan future instruction.   ☐ ☐ ☐ ☐ ☐

27. We give our students specific feedback about their learning.   ☐ ☐ ☐ ☐ ☐

28. We acknowledge students' significant achievements.   ☐ ☐ ☐ ☐ ☐

School Policies and Procedures

Respondent Role:

☐ STUDENT
☐ TEACHER
☐ ADMINISTRATOR
☐ SUPPORT STAFF (Secretary, Custodian, School Assistant, etc.)
☐ PARENT
☐ TRUSTEE
☐ COMMUNITY MEMBER (other than parent)
☐ OTHER (specify)

INSTRUCTIONS TO RESPONDENTS:

The purpose of this survey is to obtain information about what you think of certain aspects of the school giving the survey. The information will be used in an effort to improve education for students. Therefore, please read the instructions carefully and answer each question as honestly as possible. You should be able to complete this survey in about 5 minutes. Your response to the questionnaire will be anonymous and will be combined with those of others to reveal patterns. Responses from your school will be combined with responses from other schools.

We are interested in the extent to which you agree or disagree with the following statements.
For each statement, select and check ONE of the following responses:

1	2	3	4	NA
strongly agree	agree	disagree	strongly disagree	not applicable/ don't know

	strongly agree			strongly disagree	
6.1 Coherence	1	2	3	4	NA
1. Personnel selection and hiring criteria reflect our general school goals and priorities.	☐	☐	☐	☐	☐
2. The regular daily operation of our school supports achieving the school's goals.	☐	☐	☐	☐	☐
3. The school policies support achieving the school's goals.	☐	☐	☐	☐	☐
4. Our school's procedures result in responses and behaviors consistent with the school's goals.	☐	☐	☐	☐	☐
5. Routine procedures affecting the (day-to-day) school's operations support the school's priorities.	☐	☐	☐	☐	☐
6. Our school's policies and procedures are consistent with each other.	☐	☐	☐	☐	☐
7. Our school's budget allocation reflects our school's goals.	☐	☐	☐	☐	☐
6.2 Student Orientation					
8. I am expected to have high expectations of student achievement.	☐	☐	☐	☐	☐
9. I am expected to assess student progress on a regular basis.	☐	☐	☐	☐	☐
10. I am expected to assign homework on a regular basis.	☐	☐	☐	☐	☐
11. I am expected to evaluate student homework.	☐	☐	☐	☐	☐

6.3 Student Awareness

12. Students understand that they are to treat each other respectfully. □ □ □ □ □
13. Students understand that they are to treat adults respectfully. □ □ □ □ □
14. Students understand that they are to treat property respectfully. □ □ □ □ □
15. Students participate in establishing behavioral standards. □ □ □ □ □
16. Parents participate in establishing behavioral standards. □ □ □ □ □
17. School mechanisms exist to acknowledge exemplary student behavior. □ □ □ □ □

6.4 Special Needs Focus

18. Specialized programs for assisting youths in crisis are a part of the school guidance/student support program. □ □ □ □ □
19. Our school addresses the issues of equity and access for all learners. □ □ □ □ □
20. Most students with special needs are integrated with regular classes. □ □ □ □ □
21. Extra support is provided for students with special needs to be integrated with regular classes. □ □ □ □ □
22. Our school expects collaborative staff decisions regarding students with special needs. □ □ □ □ □
23. Our school provides for interaction with professionals from other agencies to help meet students' needs. □ □ □ □ □

6.5 Student Services Strategies

24. A variety of strategies is used to provide counseling services for our students (e.g., peer, individual, or group counseling; teacher-advisor programs). □ □ □ □ □
25. Teacher-advisor programs provide an effective complement to our school's professional counseling services. □ □ □ □ □
26. Peer counseling programs provide an effective complement to our school's counseling services. □ □ □ □ □
27. Homeroom classes are convened to increase students' sense of belonging. □ □ □ □ □
28. The school provides for ongoing displays of student work. □ □ □ □ □
29. The school fosters the use of "buddy" systems. □ □ □ □ □
30. School mechanisms exist to acknowledge exemplary student service. □ □ □ □ □

6.6 Professional Focus

31. Our teacher evaluation/supervision practices reflect our school goals and priorities. □ □ □ □ □
32. I have 5 or more years of experience in my work in education. □ □ □ □ □
33. I have advanced-level training in my specialty area. □ □ □ □ □
34. I have an advanced degree. □ □ □ □ □
35. Our teacher evaluation/supervision practices provide for staff development. □ □ □ □ □

6.7 Staff Development

36. Our school provides adequate release time for staff development.　☐ ☐ ☐ ☐ ☐
37. We have significant input into plans for professional development and growth.　☐ ☐ ☐ ☐ ☐
38. We assess our needs for professional development related to the process of implementing new programs.　☐ ☐ ☐ ☐ ☐
39. The process of professional growth includes opportunities to practice what we learn and then to reflect on and discuss our experiences.　☐ ☐ ☐ ☐ ☐
40. Our professional growth is facilitated with a variety of activities (e.g., observation, demonstration, discussion, practice and feedback, peer coaching).　☐ ☐ ☐ ☐ ☐
41. Our school provides formal professional development opportunities.　☐ ☐ ☐ ☐ ☐
42. Our school provides opportunities for professional development through informal working relations within this school.　☐ ☐ ☐ ☐ ☐

6.8 Resource Allocation

43. Financial resources are available when needed to facilitate teachers' own improvement initiatives.　☐ ☐ ☐ ☐ ☐
44. This school provides additional assistance for teachers responsible for classes with unusual ranges of student ability.　☐ ☐ ☐ ☐ ☐
45. This school has adequate amounts of such resources as texts, curriculum materials, and teaching aids.　☐ ☐ ☐ ☐ ☐
46. Appropriate support personnel (e.g., aides, substitutes) are available to assist in implementation of our programs.　☐ ☐ ☐ ☐ ☐
47. Allocation of resources within our school supports our school goals.　☐ ☐ ☐ ☐ ☐

School-Community Partnerships

Respondent Role:

☐ STUDENT
☐ TEACHER
☐ ADMINISTRATOR
☐ SUPPORT STAFF (Secretary, Custodian, School Assistant, etc.)
☐ PARENT
☐ TRUSTEE
☐ COMMUNITY MEMBER (other than parent)
☐ OTHER (specify)

INSTRUCTIONS TO RESPONDENTS:

The purpose of this survey is to obtain information about what you think of certain aspects of the school giving the survey. The information will be used in an effort to improve education for students. Therefore, please read the instructions carefully and answer each question as honestly as possible. You should be able to complete this survey in about 5 minutes. Your response to the questionnaire will be anonymous and will be combined with those of others to reveal patterns. Responses from your school will be combined with responses from other schools.

We are interested in the extent to which you agree or disagree with the following statements.

For each statement, select and check ONE of the following responses:

1	2	3	4	NA
strongly agree	agree	disagree	strongly disagree	not applicable/ don't know

	strongly agree			strongly disagree	
7.1 School-Community Cooperation	1	2	3	4	NA
1. Local business/industry cooperates with our school in providing cooperative educational opportunities.	☐	☐	☐	☐	☐
2. Members of the community are used as specialized resource personnel.	☐	☐	☐	☐	☐
3. Our school provides opportunities for students to become involved in the community (e.g., by using community resources or participating in community projects).	☐	☐	☐	☐	☐
4. Our school makes effective use of community resources (human and material) in providing the best possible programs for our students.	☐	☐	☐	☐	☐
5. Our school is directly involved in special community projects.	☐	☐	☐	☐	☐
6. School and community work in partnership to enhance learning for students with special needs.	☐	☐	☐	☐	☐

7.2 Postsecondary Partnerships

7. Postsecondary facilities are made available (when availability is flexible) to schools (language, computer labs).	☐	☐	☐	☐	☐
8. Postsecondary faculty have regular contact with our school members.	☐	☐	☐	☐	☐
9. Our school is aware of resources available at the postsecondary level.	☐	☐	☐	☐	☐
10. Our school has a representative who communicates regularly with faculty members at the postsecondary level.	☐	☐	☐	☐	☐
11. Special activities, such as hands-on science, experts are made available to our school to enhance the needs of the learners.	☐	☐	☐	☐	☐
12. Postsecondary faculty are used as specialized resources in regular curriculum within our school.	☐	☐	☐	☐	☐

7.3 Parent-Guardian Participation

13. Parents/guardians are involved in our school's guidance/student support program. ☐ ☐ ☐ ☐ ☐

14. Our school involves members of the community in developing educational opportunities. ☐ ☐ ☐ ☐ ☐

15. Our school promotes clear, two-way communication between school and parents/community. ☐ ☐ ☐ ☐ ☐

16. Parent/guardian-teacher interaction is encouraged. ☐ ☐ ☐ ☐ ☐

17. Parents/guardians are involved as influential decision makers in our school. ☐ ☐ ☐ ☐ ☐

18. Parents/guardians are involved in instructional roles in our school. ☐ ☐ ☐ ☐ ☐

19. Our school encourages parents to come into the school frequently to discuss their children's programs. ☐ ☐ ☐ ☐ ☐

20. Our school involves parents, after familiarization of school expectations, in support roles in the classroom. ☐ ☐ ☐ ☐ ☐

7.4 Parent-School Collaboration

21. Our school assists some parents in providing a more positive educational climate for children in their home. ☐ ☐ ☐ ☐ ☐

22. We provide parents/guardians with knowledge of techniques to assist children in learning at home. ☐ ☐ ☐ ☐ ☐

23. We take specific actions to encourage parents'/guardians' involvement in children's homework. ☐ ☐ ☐ ☐ ☐

24. Our school encourages the provision of programs to develop parenting skills, where there is a need. ☐ ☐ ☐ ☐ ☐

25. Our Parent Consultative Committee seeks ways to educate the parents in assisting children in their learning. ☐ ☐ ☐ ☐ ☐

26. Our school stresses the importance of learning being a continuation of school/home environment. ☐ ☐ ☐ ☐ ☐

7.5 Community Support Services

27. Our school provides access to community support services for children, families, and the general community. ☐ ☐ ☐ ☐ ☐

28. The community served by our school generally supports our efforts to implement new programs. ☐ ☐ ☐ ☐ ☐

29. Our school has good relations with the local media. ☐ ☐ ☐ ☐ ☐

30. Our school involves various community organizations that can enhance student learning (e.g., guest speakers). ☐ ☐ ☐ ☐ ☐

31. Our school seeks out community support services for families in need (e.g., family counseling). ☐ ☐ ☐ ☐ ☐

32. The community has developed productive ways of funding (when asked) assistance for programs in the school. ☐ ☐ ☐ ☐ ☐

Student Participation and Engagement: Family Educational Culture

I am:

☐ 11 years old or younger
☐ 12 years old
☐ 13 years old
☐ 14 years old
☐ 15 years old
☐ 16 years old
☐ 17 years old
☐ 18 years old or older

I am in grade:

☐ 7
☐ 8
☐ 9
☐ 10
☐ 11
☐ 12

☐ Male   ☐ Female

INSTRUCTIONS TO RESPONDENTS:

The purpose of this survey is to obtain information about you and how you feel about school. The information will be used in an effort to improve education for students. Therefore, please read the instructions carefully and answer each question as honestly as possible.

You should be able to complete this survey in about 20 minutes. Your response to the questionnaire will be anonymous and will be combined with those of others to reveal patterns. Responses from your school will be put together before they are combined with responses from other schools. Therefore, we would like you to print the name of your school and school district on the blanks below.

(School) _____

(District) _____

We are interested in the extent to which you agree or disagree with the following statements.

For each statement, select and check ONE of the following responses:

1	2	3	4	NA
strongly agree	agree	disagree	strongly disagree	not applicable/ don't know

Part 1: Participation in School Activities	strongly agree 1	2	3	strongly disagree 4	NA
1. I put a lot of energy into my schoolwork.	☐	☐	☐	☐	☐
2. I enjoy giving my opinion during class discussions.	☐	☐	☐	☐	☐
3. Making my own decisions about what to study helps make my schoolwork worthwhile.	☐	☐	☐	☐	☐
4. I rarely daydream in my class(es).	☐	☐	☐	☐	☐
5. In my classes, students help decide what we will do for projects and assignments.	☐	☐	☐	☐	☐
6. I frequently ask questions during class.	☐	☐	☐	☐	☐
7. I rarely am late for school.	☐	☐	☐	☐	☐
8. I always finish my schoolwork on time.	☐	☐	☐	☐	☐
9. As a student, I have helped to decide what the rules will be for our school.	☐	☐	☐	☐	☐

10. I frequently have discussions with my teachers about things that I find interesting. ☐ ☐ ☐ ☐ ☐
11. I do all the homework that I am expected to do. ☐ ☐ ☐ ☐ ☐
12. Our school's discipline rules are fair to students. ☐ ☐ ☐ ☐ ☐
13. I frequently do extra school work to find out more about something that interests me. ☐ ☐ ☐ ☐ ☐
14. I respond whenever I am asked questions during class. ☐ ☐ ☐ ☐ ☐
15. I do a lot of extra reading for my own benefit. ☐ ☐ ☐ ☐ ☐
16. My teachers encourage me to set my own goals for what I want to get out of school. ☐ ☐ ☐ ☐ ☐
17. I rarely skip class without permission. ☐ ☐ ☐ ☐ ☐
18. Participating in school events (e.g., games, dances, plays) is a very important part of my life at school. ☐ ☐ ☐ ☐ ☐
19. I have been a very active member of school clubs and/or sports teams throughout secondary school. ☐ ☐ ☐ ☐ ☐
20. On an average night during the week, I spend the following amount of time doing homework:
   ☐ none
   ☐ less than 30 minutes
   ☐ 30-60 minutes
   ☐ 1-2 hours
   ☐ more than 2 hours
21. Since the Christmas break, I have:

(For each of the following, mark the range—representing the number of days—that best describes your situation)

	0 times	1-5 times	4-10 times	more than 10 times
a. been late for school	☐	☐	☐	☐
b. skipped a class (without permission)	☐	☐	☐	☐
c. been absent for a whole day	☐	☐	☐	☐
d. been sent to the office because of misbehavior	☐	☐	☐	☐
e. had a detention	☐	☐	☐	☐
f. been suspended	☐	☐	☐	☐

Part 2: Participation in Extracurricular Activities

	always	frequently	sometimes	rarely	never	
	1	2	3	4	5	NA
1. I participate in school activities in the following ways:	☐	☐	☐	☐	☐	☐
a. As a spectator at sports events	☐	☐	☐	☐	☐	☐
b. By participating in sports events	☐	☐	☐	☐	☐	☐
c. As a spectator at other school events (e.g., plays, musicals)	☐	☐	☐	☐	☐	☐
d. By participating in our school events (e.g., plays, musicals)	☐	☐	☐	☐	☐	☐
e. By attending school dances	☐	☐	☐	☐	☐	☐
f. By participating in 1-day special events (e.g., Multicultural Day, dress-up days)	☐	☐	☐	☐	☐	☐

2. Indicate how many school organizations (e.g., sports teams, clubs—library, newspaper) you are a member of this school year.
   - ☐ 0
   - ☐ 1
   - ☐ 2-3
   - ☐ 4-5
   - ☐ 6+
3. On average, how much time per week do you spend participating in those school organizations of which you are a member?
   - ☐ 0
   - ☐ 1 hour
   - ☐ 2-4 hours
   - ☐ 5-8 hours
   - ☐ 9+

	strongly agree 1	2	3	strongly disagree 4	NA
Part 3: View on Education					
1. The most important things that happen to me usually happen at school.	☐	☐	☐	☐	☐
2. I think schoolwork is really important.	☐	☐	☐	☐	☐
3. My parents/guardians make sure I do my homework before having free time.	☐	☐	☐	☐	☐
4. It is really important to me that I gain knowledge and develop skills through my schoolwork.	☐	☐	☐	☐	☐
5. I like the way teachers teach in most of my classes.	☐	☐	☐	☐	☐
6. I am proud of my school.	☐	☐	☐	☐	☐
7. I really enjoy school most of the time.	☐	☐	☐	☐	☐
8. All people should get as much education as they can.	☐	☐	☐	☐	☐
9. My school gives me access to books and equipment that I need.	☐	☐	☐	☐	☐
10. I am constantly challenged in class.	☐	☐	☐	☐	☐
11. My schoolwork is helping me prepare for life after I finish school.	☐	☐	☐	☐	☐
12. Most of my teachers relate schoolwork to my future life.	☐	☐	☐	☐	☐
13. My teachers use a variety of activities in my classes.	☐	☐	☐	☐	☐
14. My parents/guardians encourage me to participate in extracurricular activities and events.	☐	☐	☐	☐	☐
15. We have the right number of quizzes, tests, and exams in my courses.	☐	☐	☐	☐	☐
16. The things I learn in school are useful in my life outside school.	☐	☐	☐	☐	☐
17. My parents/guardians always know whether or not I am at school.	☐	☐	☐	☐	☐
18. My parents/guardians usually go to parents' nights and special school events.	☐	☐	☐	☐	☐
Part 4: Views on Atmosphere for Learning					
1. Most of my classes are well organized.	☐	☐	☐	☐	☐
2. Most of my teachers go out of their way to help students.	☐	☐	☐	☐	☐
3. School spirit is very high in my school.	☐	☐	☐	☐	☐
4. I feel that I "belong" at this school.	☐	☐	☐	☐	☐
5. Most of my teachers are interested in me as a person.	☐	☐	☐	☐	☐

6. I have made many friends in my school. □ □ □ □ □
7. My teachers frequently discuss my work with me. □ □ □ □ □
8. I often discuss my schoolwork with my parents/guardians. □ □ □ □ □
9. Most of my teachers treat me the same as other students. □ □ □ □ □
10. Most of my teachers are willing to spend extra time with me. □ □ □ □ □
11. Most of my teachers expect me always to do my best work. □ □ □ □ □
12. Most of my teachers make me feel comfortable in class. □ □ □ □ □
13. Study aids at home (e.g., books, an encyclopedia, magazines, computer) help me do better schoolwork. □ □ □ □ □
14. I have come to know other students in our school really well. □ □ □ □ □
15. I get along with most other students I have met in my school. □ □ □ □ □
16. My parents/guardians always are willing to help me with my schoolwork. □ □ □ □ □
17. My teachers spend time just talking with me. □ □ □ □ □
18. Most of my teachers seem to understand me. □ □ □ □ □
19. I often have conversations about major world events with my parents/guardians. □ □ □ □ □
20. I get along with most of my teachers. □ □ □ □ □
21. I have my own work space at home that is fairly quiet for doing homework and school projects. □ □ □ □ □
22. My parents/guardians ensure that I have a healthy diet and enough sleep. □ □ □ □ □

Part 5: Views on My Schoolwork

1. I am able to understand most of the material covered in my classes. □ □ □ □ □
2. I feel confident that I will be successful in school. □ □ □ □ □
3. I am learning a lot at school. □ □ □ □ □
4. I will graduate from high school. □ □ □ □ □
5. I am satisfied with my marks. □ □ □ □ □

Appendix B:
The District Surveys

This section includes survey instruments for measuring the current status of a school district. The nine surveys in this section are as follows:

- District Mission and Goals
- District Culture
- District Core Tasks (three instruments about different aspects of the core tasks)
- District Structure and Organization
- District Information Collection and Decision Making
- District Policies and Procedures
- District-Community Partnerships

Each of these instruments is quite brief and should require less than 15 minutes to complete.

District Mission and Goals

Respondent Role:

☐ STUDENT
☐ TEACHER
☐ ADMINISTRATOR
☐ SUPPORT STAFF (Secretary, Custodian, School Assistant, etc.)
☐ PARENT
☐ TRUSTEE
☐ COMMUNITY MEMBER (other than parent)
☐ OTHER (specify)

INSTRUCTIONS TO RESPONDENTS:

The purpose of this survey is to obtain information about what you think of certain aspects of the district giving the survey. The information will be used in an effort to improve education for students. Therefore, please read the instructions carefully and answer each question as honestly as possible. You should be able to complete this survey in about 5 minutes. Your response to the questionnaire will be anonymous and will be combined with those of others to reveal patterns. Responses from your school will be combined with responses from other schools.

We are interested in the extent to which you agree or disagree with the following statements.

For each statement, select and check ONE of the following responses:

1	2	3	4	NA
strongly agree	agree	disagree	strongly disagree	not applicable/ don't know

	strongly agree			strongly disagree	
1.1 Clarity	1	2	3	4	NA
1. I have a clear understanding of the district's goals.	☐	☐	☐	☐	☐
2. I have a clear understanding of the district's mission statement.	☐	☐	☐	☐	☐
3. Our district mission statement is easily understood by staff.	☐	☐	☐	☐	☐
4. Our district goals are easily understood by staff.	☐	☐	☐	☐	☐
1.2 Meaningfulness					
5. Our district mission statement is significant.	☐	☐	☐	☐	☐
6. Our district goals are significant.	☐	☐	☐	☐	☐
7. I consider our district goals to be worth extra effort to achieve.	☐	☐	☐	☐	☐
1.3 Awareness					
8. I am aware of the district's mission statement.	☐	☐	☐	☐	☐
9. I am aware of the district's goals.	☐	☐	☐	☐	☐
10. Most staff are aware of our district mission and goals.	☐	☐	☐	☐	☐

1.4 Usefulness

11. District goals and mission statement influence decisions at the school level. □ □ □ □ □
12. District goals and mission statement influence decisions at the district level. □ □ □ □ □

1.5 Currency

13. Our district mission statement is reviewed periodically. □ □ □ □ □
14. Our district mission statement is revised periodically. □ □ □ □ □
15. Our district goals are reviewed periodically. □ □ □ □ □
16. Our district goals are revised periodically. □ □ □ □ □

1.6 Congruence

17. Our district goals are compatible with state/provincial goals. □ □ □ □ □
18. Our district mission statement is compatible with the state/provincial
    mission statement. □ □ □ □ □

District Culture

Respondent Role:

☐ STUDENT
☐ TEACHER
☐ ADMINISTRATOR
☐ SUPPORT STAFF (Secretary, Custodian, School Assistant, etc.)
☐ PARENT
☐ TRUSTEE
☐ COMMUNITY MEMBER (other than parent)
☐ OTHER (specify)

INSTRUCTIONS TO RESPONDENTS:

The purpose of this survey is to obtain information about what you think of certain aspects of the district giving the survey. The information will be used in an effort to improve education for students. Therefore, please read the instructions carefully and answer each question as honestly as possible. You should be able to complete this survey in about 5 minutes. Your response to the questionnaire will be anonymous and will be combined with those of others to reveal patterns. Responses from your school will be combined with responses from other schools.

We are interested in the extent to which you agree or disagree with the following statements.

For each statement, select and check ONE of the following responses:

1	2	3	4	NA
strongly agree	agree	disagree	strongly disagree	not applicable/ don't know

	strongly agree			strongly disagree	
2.1 Norms	1	2	3	4	NA
1. Administrative officers support and encourage professional growth for all staff.	☐	☐	☐	☐	☐
2. All employees are made to feel that they are making a valued contribution to the achievement of district goals.	☐	☐	☐	☐	☐
3. Good working relations are evident among all district employees.	☐	☐	☐	☐	☐
4. Our district expects high levels of performance from students.	☐	☐	☐	☐	☐
5. Our district expects high levels of performance from all staff.	☐	☐	☐	☐	☐
6. I am made to feel that my contribution matters within this district.	☐	☐	☐	☐	☐
7. Relationships among different staff groups are characterized by mutual respect.	☐	☐	☐	☐	☐
8. Our district has relatively few labor relations problems.	☐	☐	☐	☐	☐

2.2 Beliefs

9. It is important that all employees be aware of our district's mission and goals.	☐	☐	☐	☐	☐
10. My knowledge of the district's mission and goals influences my job.	☐	☐	☐	☐	☐
11. Most staff in our district assume that all students can benefit from an education.	☐	☐	☐	☐	☐
12. Change and improvement are necessary in my job.	☐	☐	☐	☐	☐
13. In our district, continuous improvement is viewed as a necessary part of every job by most staff.	☐	☐	☐	☐	☐
14. I have confidence in the integrity of my colleagues.	☐	☐	☐	☐	☐

2.3 Values

15. I have a responsibility to contribute to all decisions related to my job. ☐ ☐ ☐ ☐ ☐
16. All employees are aware of their duties and responsibilities. ☐ ☐ ☐ ☐ ☐
17. Decisions are made by appropriate personnel in our district. ☐ ☐ ☐ ☐ ☐
18. The consequences of decisions on students and others are always considered before decisions are made final. ☐ ☐ ☐ ☐ ☐

2.4 Assumptions

19. The students' welfare is of paramount importance in all district decisions. ☐ ☐ ☐ ☐ ☐
20. The community's needs are of paramount importance in district decision making. ☐ ☐ ☐ ☐ ☐
21. There is frequent, worthwhile communication between school, district, and community groups. ☐ ☐ ☐ ☐ ☐
22. The community is a valued partner in the decision-making process. ☐ ☐ ☐ ☐ ☐
23. The district is accountable to the community for its decisions. ☐ ☐ ☐ ☐ ☐

2.5 Forms of Culture

24. All stakeholders in our district have a role to play in the decision-making process. ☐ ☐ ☐ ☐ ☐
25. The physical condition of district schools mirrors district goals. ☐ ☐ ☐ ☐ ☐
26. Conflict within our district is resolved in a fair and equitable manner. ☐ ☐ ☐ ☐ ☐
27. We recognize that some issues within our district will be left unresolved. ☐ ☐ ☐ ☐ ☐

District Core Tasks (a)

Respondent Role:

☐ STUDENT

☐ TEACHER

☐ ADMINISTRATOR

☐ SUPPORT STAFF (Secretary, Custodian, School Assistant, etc.)

☐ PARENT

☐ TRUSTEE

☐ COMMUNITY MEMBER (other than parent)

☐ OTHER (specify)

INSTRUCTIONS TO RESPONDENTS:

The purpose of this survey is to obtain information about what you think of certain aspects of the district giving the survey. The information will be used in an effort to improve education for students. Therefore, please read the instructions carefully and answer each question as honestly as possible. You should be able to complete this survey in about 5 minutes. Your response to the questionnaire will be anonymous and will be combined with those of others to reveal patterns. Responses from your school will be combined with responses from other schools.

We are interested in the extent to which you agree or disagree with the following statements.

For each statement, select and check ONE of the following responses:

1	2	3	4	NA
strongly agree	agree	disagree	strongly disagree	not applicable/ don't know

	strongly agree			strongly disagree	
3.1.1 Strategic Planning—Influences on plan	1	2	3	4	NA
1. Representation of stakeholder groups on major committees is proportional.	☐	☐	☐	☐	☐
2. The school improvement planning process is a major source of information for strategic planning.	☐	☐	☐	☐	☐
3. All stakeholder groups in our district have an opportunity to influence the strategic plan.	☐	☐	☐	☐	☐
3.1.2 Strategic Planning—Review of current status					
4. Data about district operations are collected systematically.	☐	☐	☐	☐	☐
5. Changes are made to the strategic plan when data indicate stakeholder needs are not being met.	☐	☐	☐	☐	☐
6. Data on district operations are reviewed regularly to determine progress in achieving district goals.	☐	☐	☐	☐	☐
3.1.3 Strategic Planning—Systematic trend analyses					
7. Future trend analysis is part of the strategic planning process in our district.	☐	☐	☐	☐	☐
8. Historical trends and past practices are considered during our strategic planning process.	☐	☐	☐	☐	☐
9. Relevant state/provincial trends are considered during our district strategic planning process.	☐	☐	☐	☐	☐

10. Relevant national trends are considered during our district strategic planning process. □ □ □ □ □

11. Relevant global trends are considered during our district strategic planning process. □ □ □ □ □

3.1.4 Strategic Planning—Goal sources

12. School goals are a source of district goals. □ □ □ □ □
13. Parental aspirations are a source of district goals. □ □ □ □ □
14. State/provincial priorities are a source of district goals. □ □ □ □ □
15. Political realities are a source of district goals. □ □ □ □ □

3.1.5 Strategic Planning—Support and awareness

16. I understand our district strategic plan. □ □ □ □ □
17. I agree with our district strategic plan. □ □ □ □ □
18. All stakeholder groups in our district are aware of the strategic planning process. □ □ □ □ □
19. I agree with the process used to develop our strategic plan. □ □ □ □ □
20. I am aware of how our strategic plan was developed. □ □ □ □ □
21. All stakeholder groups in our district are informed of the outcomes of the strategic planning process. □ □ □ □ □
22. Most stakeholder groups in our district agree with our strategic plan. □ □ □ □ □

3.1.6 Strategic Planning—Relation to district goals

23. Our school improvement plan uses the strategic plan as an important source of direction. □ □ □ □ □
24. A significant amount of time has been spent discussing district goals in my school. □ □ □ □ □
25. Goals developed during district strategic planning provide a compelling framework for goal setting in our school. □ □ □ □ □

3.1.7 Strategic Planning—Monitoring process

26. The monitoring process for our district is clearly understandable. □ □ □ □ □
27. Portions of our district strategic plan are monitored annually. □ □ □ □ □
28. Results of our district monitoring process lead me to review my own practices. □ □ □ □ □
29. Results of our district monitoring process are used to improve the district strategic plan. □ □ □ □ □
30. Measures of student progress are used to monitor the effectiveness of the district strategic plan. □ □ □ □ □
31. The results of the monitoring process stimulate significant improvements in the district. □ □ □ □ □
32. Our district has implemented an effective process for monitoring progress in achieving its goals. □ □ □ □ □

3.1.8 Strategic Planning—Evaluating effectiveness

33. Our district evaluates the effectiveness of its strategic planning process.   □   □   □   □   □
34. The strategic planning process enables the district to achieve its mission.   □   □   □   □   □
35. The strategic planning process reflects the mission of the district.   □   □   □   □   □
36. The process for monitoring the strategic plan is effective.   □   □   □   □   □

3.1.9 Strategic Planning—Data bank use

37. The process for monitoring the progress of our district strategic plan produces a data bank about district functioning.   □   □   □   □   □
38. Data collected about the school district functioning are available to me.   □   □   □   □   □
39. Data collected about the school district functioning are useful to me.   □   □   □   □   □
40. Data collected about progress with the district plan are useful in improving classroom instruction.   □   □   □   □   □
41. Data collected about progress with the district plan are useful in school improvement plans.   □   □   □   □   □
42. Data collected about progress with the district plan are useful for many purposes.   □   □   □   □   □

3.1.10 Strategic Planning—Planning process outcomes

43. Outcomes of the strategic planning process are communicated regularly to all stakeholders.   □   □   □   □   □
44. Relevant information about the strategic planning process is communicated regularly to all stakeholders.   □   □   □   □   □
45. Communications regarding the strategic planning processes and outcomes are effective.   □   □   □   □   □

District Core Tasks (b)

Respondent Role:

☐ STUDENT

☐ TEACHER

☐ ADMINISTRATOR

☐ SUPPORT STAFF (Secretary, Custodian, School Assistant, etc.)

☐ PARENT

☐ TRUSTEE

☐ COMMUNITY MEMBER (other than parent)

☐ OTHER (specify)

INSTRUCTIONS TO RESPONDENTS:

The purpose of this survey is to obtain information about what you think of certain aspects of the district giving the survey. The information will be used in an effort to improve education for students. Therefore, please read the instructions carefully and answer each question as honestly as possible. You should be able to complete this survey in about 5 minutes. Your response to the questionnaire will be anonymous and will be combined with those of others to reveal patterns. Responses from your school will be combined with responses from other schools.

We are interested in the extent to which you agree or disagree with the following statements.

For each statement, select and check ONE of the following responses:

1	2	3	4	NA
strongly agree	agree	disagree	strongly disagree	not applicable/ don't know

	strongly agree			strongly disagree	
3.2.1 Management of District Operations—Operational planning	1	2	3	4	NA
1. Each district department's operational plan defines how that team will help achieve the district strategic plan.	☐	☐	☐	☐	☐
2. Each district department's operational plan defines that team's contribution to district maintenance.	☐	☐	☐	☐	☐
3. Each district department's operational plan defines how that team will provide service to the schools.	☐	☐	☐	☐	☐
4. Each district department regularly reviews and refines its operational plan.	☐	☐	☐	☐	☐
3.2.2 Management of District Operations—Organizing					
5. There are high levels of coherence between the jobs of district department members and the way their units are organized.	☐	☐	☐	☐	☐
3.2.3 Management of District Operations—Staffing					
6. Staffing practices of the district reflect the district mission statement.	☐	☐	☐	☐	☐
7. Staffing practices demonstrate shared leadership responsibilities among teachers, administrators, and district staff.	☐	☐	☐	☐	☐
8. District staffing practices provide for "excellence" in staffing, rather than "barely adequate."	☐	☐	☐	☐	☐
9. District hiring criteria encourage commitment to district mission and goals.	☐	☐	☐	☐	☐
10. District staff development activities encourage commitment to district mission and goals.	☐	☐	☐	☐	☐

3.2.4 Management of District Operations—Supervision and evaluation

11. Our district ensures clear communication of evaluative criteria to those being evaluated.   □   □   □   □   □
12. Our district uses results of performance review in staff development planning.   □   □   □   □   □
13. The process used to monitor staff performance is sensitive to the level of responsibility of the specific position being monitored.   □   □   □   □   □
14. District supervision/evaluation criteria include measures of staff accountability.   □   □   □   □   □

3.2.5 Management of District Operations—Coordination

15. The operational plans of district departments are consistent in supporting the district strategic plan.   □   □   □   □   □
16. The efforts of district departments are consistent in supporting district policies.   □   □   □   □   □

3.2.6 Management of District Operations—Communication

17. Members of district departments have a detailed understanding of how their work relates to that of other departments.   □   □   □   □   □
18. Communication among district departments is encouraged to ensure that their combined efforts contribute to the district strategic plan.   □   □   □   □   □

3.2.7 Management of District Operations—Budgeting

19. District financial resources are allocated according to priorities identified in the district planning processes.   □   □   □   □   □
20. Budgeting decisions reflect district mission and goals.   □   □   □   □   □

District Core Tasks (c)

Respondent Role:

☐ STUDENT
☐ TEACHER
☐ ADMINISTRATOR
☐ SUPPORT STAFF (Secretary, Custodian, School Assistant, etc.)
☐ PARENT
☐ TRUSTEE
☐ COMMUNITY MEMBER (other than parent)
☐ OTHER (specify)

INSTRUCTIONS TO RESPONDENTS:

The purpose of this survey is to obtain information about what you think of certain aspects of the district giving the survey. The information will be used in an effort to improve education for students. Therefore, please read the instructions carefully and answer each question as honestly as possible. You should be able to complete this survey in about 5 minutes. Your response to the questionnaire will be anonymous and will be combined with those of others to reveal patterns. Responses from your school will be combined with responses from other schools.

We are interested in the extent to which you agree or disagree with the following statements.

For each statement, select and check ONE of the following responses:

1	2	3	4	NA
strongly agree	agree	disagree	strongly disagree	not applicable/ don't know

	strongly agree			strongly disagree	
3.3.1 District Leadership—Provides vision and/or inspiration	1	2	3	4	NA
1. District leaders have the capacity and judgment to overcome most obstacles.	☐	☐	☐	☐	☐
2. District leaders inspire staff to cooperate by demonstrating the advantages of working as a group.	☐	☐	☐	☐	☐
3. District leaders assist staff in developing goals that meet their needs.	☐	☐	☐	☐	☐
4. District leaders give staff an overall sense of purpose.	☐	☐	☐	☐	☐
3.3.2 District Leadership—Models behavior					
5. District leaders lead as much by "doing" as by "telling."	☐	☐	☐	☐	☐
6. District leaders symbolize success and accomplishment within the profession.	☐	☐	☐	☐	☐
7. District leaders provide good models for staff to follow.	☐	☐	☐	☐	☐
8. District leaders visit schools on a regular basis.	☐	☐	☐	☐	☐
9. District leaders maintain high professional behavior.	☐	☐	☐	☐	☐
3.3.3 District Leadership—Provides individualized support					
10. District leaders assist staff members in finding resources to accomplish their goals.	☐	☐	☐	☐	☐
11. District leaders treat staff members as professionals with unique needs and capacities.	☐	☐	☐	☐	☐
12. District leaders respect individual opinions when introducing changes that affect their work.	☐	☐	☐	☐	☐
13. District leaders are thoughtful of personal needs of staff members.	☐	☐	☐	☐	☐
14. District leaders provide specialists to assist staff members in accomplishing their goals.	☐	☐	☐	☐	☐

3.3.4 District Leadership—Provides intellectual stimulation

15. District leaders encourage staff to continually update and modify their skills. ☐ ☐ ☐ ☐ ☐
16. District leaders stimulate staff to develop and implement district/school goals. ☐ ☐ ☐ ☐ ☐
17. District leaders provide workshops to help staff carry out their tasks more effectively. ☐ ☐ ☐ ☐ ☐
18. District leaders provide for continuous training of staff to develop their skills. ☐ ☐ ☐ ☐ ☐
19. District leaders encourage staff to enroll in postsecondary courses by providing funds. ☐ ☐ ☐ ☐ ☐

3.3.5 District Leadership—Fosters commitment to group goals

20. District leaders encourage staff to work cooperatively for the same goals. ☐ ☐ ☐ ☐ ☐
21. District leaders encourage school staff to develop school goals that are consistent with district goals. ☐ ☐ ☐ ☐ ☐
22. District leaders help staff get involved in implementing district goals. ☐ ☐ ☐ ☐ ☐
23. District leaders provide time for staff to regularly monitor progress toward group goals. ☐ ☐ ☐ ☐ ☐
24. District leaders work at helping school staff appreciate district mission and goals. ☐ ☐ ☐ ☐ ☐

3.3.6 District Leadership—Encourages high performance

25. District leadership provides staff development programs to enhance staff performance. ☐ ☐ ☐ ☐ ☐
26. District leaders assist staffs' performance through the evaluation process. ☐ ☐ ☐ ☐ ☐
27. District leaders involve staff in leadership roles. ☐ ☐ ☐ ☐ ☐

3.3.7 District Leadership—Provides contingent reward

28. District leadership frequently acknowledges our performance. ☐ ☐ ☐ ☐ ☐
29. District leadership pays us personal compliments for our work. ☐ ☐ ☐ ☐ ☐
30. District leadership provides recognition for special work. ☐ ☐ ☐ ☐ ☐
31. District leadership helps us get those resources we decide we want. ☐ ☐ ☐ ☐ ☐
32. District leadership uses a reward system for professional improvement. ☐ ☐ ☐ ☐ ☐

3.3.8 District Leadership—Encourages individual improvement

33. District leaders encourage staff to strive continually to be better. ☐ ☐ ☐ ☐ ☐
34. District leaders provide individuals with the information they need to improve their own capability. ☐ ☐ ☐ ☐ ☐
35. District leaders encourage people to take initiative. ☐ ☐ ☐ ☐ ☐

District Structure and Organization

Respondent Role:

☐ STUDENT

☐ TEACHER

☐ ADMINISTRATOR

☐ SUPPORT STAFF (Secretary, Custodian, School Assistant, etc.)

☐ PARENT

☐ TRUSTEE

☐ COMMUNITY MEMBER (other than parent)

☐ OTHER (specify)

INSTRUCTIONS TO RESPONDENTS:

The purpose of this survey is to obtain information about what you think of certain aspects of the district giving the survey. The information will be used in an effort to improve education for students. Therefore, please read the instructions carefully and answer each question as honestly as possible. You should be able to complete this survey in about 5 minutes. Your response to the questionnaire will be anonymous and will be combined with those of others to reveal patterns. Responses from your school will be combined with responses from other schools.

We are interested in the extent to which you agree or disagree with the following statements.

For each statement, select and check ONE of the following responses:

1	2	3	4	NA
strongly agree	agree	disagree	strongly disagree	not applicable/ don't know

	strongly agree			strongly disagree	
4.1 Monitoring Decentralization	1	2	3	4	NA
1. Our district has a well-developed plan for decentralization of decision making.	☐	☐	☐	☐	☐
2. Our district decentralization plan clarifies decisions to be centralized.	☐	☐	☐	☐	☐
3. Our district decentralization plan assesses the extent of support to further decentralization.	☐	☐	☐	☐	☐
4. Our district has an effective mechanism to monitor decentralization of decision making.	☐	☐	☐	☐	☐
5. Our district has an effective mechanism to revise its decentralization process.	☐	☐	☐	☐	☐
6. Our district is monitoring the impact of decentralization on school decision making.	☐	☐	☐	☐	☐
7. Our district is monitoring the impact of decentralization on the accountability of schools.	☐	☐	☐	☐	☐
8. Our district is monitoring the impact of decentralization on district productivity.	☐	☐	☐	☐	☐

4.2 Effectiveness of Structures

	1	2	3	4	NA
9. The organizational structures of the district facilitate the day-to-day work of all staff groups.	☐	☐	☐	☐	☐
10. The structure of the district departments is helpful to day-to-day work.	☐	☐	☐	☐	☐
11. The structure of the Human Resources Department is helpful to day-to-day work.	☐	☐	☐	☐	☐
12. The structure of the Facilities Department is helpful to day-to-day work.	☐	☐	☐	☐	☐
13. The voice-answering service is helpful to day-to-day work.	☐	☐	☐	☐	☐
14. The electronic mail service is helpful to day-to-day work.	☐	☐	☐	☐	☐

4.3 Collaboration and Communication

15. Our district's organizational structures facilitate collaboration among different staff groups. □ □ □ □ □
16. Our district facilitates collaboration among schools. □ □ □ □ □
17. I am encouraged to collaborate with district department staff. □ □ □ □ □
18. I can communicate easily with most other members of our district. □ □ □ □ □
19. I have frequent opportunities to communicate with other members of our district. □ □ □ □ □
20. I am encouraged to acquire new knowledge from outside our district. □ □ □ □ □
21. I can easily obtain information that I might need from within the organization. □ □ □ □ □

4.4 Facilitation of Alternative Practices

22. I am encouraged to consider using a wide range of practices in my work. □ □ □ □ □
23. Our district establishes informal teacher groups to consider alternative educational practices. □ □ □ □ □
24. Our district involves staff members on formal committees that consider alternative approaches for education. □ □ □ □ □
25. I am encouraged to consider alternative points of view within my school setting. □ □ □ □ □
26. I am encouraged to work informally with others in exploring alternative points of view on educational practices. □ □ □ □ □
27. I am encouraged to participate on formal committees to explore alternative points of view on educational practices. □ □ □ □ □

4.5 Provision of School Autonomy

28. My school makes significant decisions regarding the generation of its goals. □ □ □ □ □
29. My school makes significant decisions regarding the implementation of its goals. □ □ □ □ □
30. My school is accountable for the outcomes of its goals. □ □ □ □ □
31. My school's goals reflect the needs of its student community. □ □ □ □ □
32. My school's goals reflect the needs of its parent community. □ □ □ □ □
33. District support to my school reflects the school's unique needs. □ □ □ □ □
34. Our district supports variation in programs and services from school to school. □ □ □ □ □

District Information Collection and Decision Making

Respondent Role:

☐ STUDENT
☐ TEACHER
☐ ADMINISTRATOR
☐ SUPPORT STAFF (Secretary, Custodian, School Assistant, etc.)
☐ PARENT
☐ TRUSTEE
☐ COMMUNITY MEMBER (other than parent)
☐ OTHER (specify)

INSTRUCTIONS TO RESPONDENTS:

The purpose of this survey is to obtain information about what you think of certain aspects of the district giving the survey. The information will be used in an effort to improve education for students. Therefore, please read the instructions carefully and answer each question as honestly as possible. You should be able to complete this survey in about 5 minutes. Your response to the questionnaire will be anonymous and will be combined with those of others to reveal patterns. Responses from your school will be combined with responses from other schools.

We are interested in the extent to which you agree or disagree with the following statements.

For each statement, select and check ONE of the following responses:

1	2	3	4	NA
strongly agree	agree	disagree	strongly disagree	not applicable/ don't know

	strongly agree			strongly disagree	
5.1 Information Sources	1	2	3	4	NA
1. A systematic, districtwide student assessment program is in place.	☐	☐	☐	☐	☐
2. Our district systematically monitors the progress of school improvement plans.	☐	☐	☐	☐	☐
3. Our district maintains a computerized data bank of relevant information about individual students.	☐	☐	☐	☐	☐
4. Our district keeps an up-to-date record of staff qualifications and experience (computer).	☐	☐	☐	☐	☐
5. Our district gathers information about the socioeconomic climate of the district in order to make appropriate decisions.	☐	☐	☐	☐	☐
6. Our district maintains up-to-date information on changing trends in parent/ community concerns.	☐	☐	☐	☐	☐
5.2 Use of Information					
7. Our district incorporates student assessment data into all appropriate decisions.	☐	☐	☐	☐	☐
8. Our district uses information on special needs of students to make appropriate decisions.	☐	☐	☐	☐	☐
9. Our district provides consultative committees at the school with a variety of school-specific information.	☐	☐	☐	☐	☐
10. Our staff use district information to help formulate decisions for our school.	☐	☐	☐	☐	☐
11. Appropriate use of district information is determined through discussions with school administrators.	☐	☐	☐	☐	☐

5.3 Information for Organizational Learning

12. Our district fosters the flow of ideas into and throughout the district. ☐ ☐ ☐ ☐ ☐

13. Our district provides opportunities for teachers and administrators to share knowledge informally. ☐ ☐ ☐ ☐ ☐

14. Open communication facilitates sharing relevant facts and feelings through the district. ☐ ☐ ☐ ☐ ☐

15. Ample opportunities are provided for discussion of ideas among different staff groups. ☐ ☐ ☐ ☐ ☐

5.4 Forms of Decision Making

16. All stakeholder groups participate in significant district-level decisions. ☐ ☐ ☐ ☐ ☐

17. Decision making in our district takes place where the decisions will be implemented. ☐ ☐ ☐ ☐ ☐

18. District mission and goals are used as criteria for decision making. ☐ ☐ ☐ ☐ ☐

19. Our district has adopted a longer term perspective for decision making than the annual cycle. ☐ ☐ ☐ ☐ ☐

20. Procedures for decision making in our district are reasonable and clear. ☐ ☐ ☐ ☐ ☐

5.5 Problem Solving

21. In our district, problems are viewed as issues to be solved or circumvented. ☐ ☐ ☐ ☐ ☐

22. In our district, problems are not viewed as barriers to action. ☐ ☐ ☐ ☐ ☐

23. In our district, problems are perceived to provide potential opportunities for reaching important objectives. ☐ ☐ ☐ ☐ ☐

District Policies and Procedures

Respondent Role:

☐ STUDENT
☐ TEACHER
☐ ADMINISTRATOR
☐ SUPPORT STAFF (Secretary, Custodian, School Assistant, etc.)
☐ PARENT
☐ TRUSTEE
☐ COMMUNITY MEMBER (other than parent)
☐ OTHER (specify)

INSTRUCTIONS TO RESPONDENTS:

The purpose of this survey is to obtain information about what you think of certain aspects of the district giving the survey. The information will be used in an effort to improve education for students. Therefore, please read the instructions carefully and answer each question as honestly as possible. You should be able to complete this survey in about 5 minutes. Your response to the questionnaire will be anonymous and will be combined with those of others to reveal patterns. Responses from your school will be combined with responses from other schools.

We are interested in the extent to which you agree or disagree with the following statements.

For each statement, select and check ONE of the following responses:

1	2	3	4	NA
strongly agree	agree	disagree	strongly disagree	not applicable/ don't know

	strongly agree			strongly disagree	
6.1 Orientation of Policies and Procedures	1	2	3	4	NA
1. Clear rules and guidelines for school operation are provided by the district.	☐	☐	☐	☐	☐
2. Schools are encouraged to implement district rules and guidelines flexibly.	☐	☐	☐	☐	☐
3. Schools have sufficient opportunity for input into district policies and procedures.	☐	☐	☐	☐	☐
4. Schools have sufficient discretion in the implementing of district policies and procedures.	☐	☐	☐	☐	☐
5. A balance exists between district and school control over district goals.	☐	☐	☐	☐	☐
6. A balance exists between district and school control over assessment of district goals.	☐	☐	☐	☐	☐

6.2 System Coherence

7. District policies and procedures recognize that student learning supersedes administrative convenience.	☐	☐	☐	☐	☐
8. District policies and procedures facilitate achievement of our school goals.	☐	☐	☐	☐	☐
9. District policies and procedures facilitate achievement of district goals.	☐	☐	☐	☐	☐
10. District policies and procedures are compatible with each other.	☐	☐	☐	☐	☐

6.3.1 Facilitation of Staff Development

11. District-sponsored staff development reflects district goals. ☐ ☐ ☐ ☐ ☐
12. Our district makes available a broad range of staff development opportunities. ☐ ☐ ☐ ☐ ☐
13. Our district facilitates sufficient on-site professional development for teachers. ☐ ☐ ☐ ☐ ☐
14. Our district facilitates sufficient out-of-school staff development for teachers. ☐ ☐ ☐ ☐ ☐
15. Adequate release time is available for staff development. ☐ ☐ ☐ ☐ ☐
16. Our district facilitates sufficient off-site professional development for administrators. ☐ ☐ ☐ ☐ ☐
17. Our district facilitates sufficient on-site professional development for administrators. ☐ ☐ ☐ ☐ ☐

6.3.2 Evaluation of Administrators and Teachers

18. District staff evaluation policies reflect a commitment to growth. ☐ ☐ ☐ ☐ ☐
19. District staff evaluation policies are based on clear criteria. ☐ ☐ ☐ ☐ ☐
20. District staff evaluation policies are tied to district and school goals. ☐ ☐ ☐ ☐ ☐
21. District staff evaluation policies are consistent with research on effective practice. ☐ ☐ ☐ ☐ ☐
22. Administrators are rewarded for fostering the professional growth of those they administer. ☐ ☐ ☐ ☐ ☐
23. Administrators are rewarded for creating effective work groups. ☐ ☐ ☐ ☐ ☐
24. Evidence about staff performance is based on the regular collection of several forms of information. ☐ ☐ ☐ ☐ ☐
25. Our collective bargaining agreements regard evaluation as an opportunity for professional growth. ☐ ☐ ☐ ☐ ☐
26. The district evaluation process allows time for conferencing, observation, and feedback. ☐ ☐ ☐ ☐ ☐
27. District resources are made available for evaluation. ☐ ☐ ☐ ☐ ☐
28. Evaluators are perceived to be a credible source of ideas. ☐ ☐ ☐ ☐ ☐
29. Evaluators are perceived to be worthy of trust. ☐ ☐ ☐ ☐ ☐
30. Evaluators provide a supportive model of change. ☐ ☐ ☐ ☐ ☐

6.3.3 Encouragement of Effective Instruction

31. Districtwide instructional goals have been established.
32. Our district encourages teachers to choose strategies based on instructional goals. ☐ ☐ ☐ ☐ ☐
33. Our district encourages teachers to choose strategies based on student characteristics. ☐ ☐ ☐ ☐ ☐
34. The acquisition of a large repertoire of teaching strategies is promoted by district policy. ☐ ☐ ☐ ☐ ☐

6.3.4 School Improvement Process

35. The district provides clear guidelines for school improvement. ☐ ☐ ☐ ☐ ☐
36. A school planning process is mandated for all schools in our district. ☐ ☐ ☐ ☐ ☐
37. School planning reflects district planning. ☐ ☐ ☐ ☐ ☐

District-Community Partnerships

Respondent Role:

☐ STUDENT

☐ TEACHER

☐ ADMINISTRATOR

☐ SUPPORT STAFF (Secretary, Custodian, School Assistant, etc.)

☐ PARENT

☐ TRUSTEE

☐ COMMUNITY MEMBER (other than parent)

☐ OTHER (specify)

INSTRUCTIONS TO RESPONDENTS:

The purpose of this survey is to obtain information about what you think of certain aspects of the district giving the survey. The information will be used in an effort to improve education for students. Therefore, please read the instructions carefully and answer each question as honestly as possible. You should be able to complete this survey in about 5 minutes. Your response to the questionnaire will be anonymous and will be combined with those of others to reveal patterns. Responses from your school will be combined with responses from other schools.

We are interested in the extent to which you agree or disagree with the following statements.

For each statement, select and check ONE of the following responses:

1	2	3	4	NA
strongly agree	agree	disagree	strongly disagree	not applicable/ don't know

	strongly agree			strongly disagree	
7.1 District-Community Relationships	1	2	3	4	NA
1. Local media report positively on district activities.	☐	☐	☐	☐	☐
2. Strong, negative advocacy groups are not active in our district.	☐	☐	☐	☐	☐
3. Cooperative ventures exist between businesses and schools/district.	☐	☐	☐	☐	☐
4. A good rapport exists between the district and the community at large.	☐	☐	☐	☐	☐
5. The community endorses district activities.	☐	☐	☐	☐	☐
6. Our senior administration has a positive relationship with the state/ provincial government.	☐	☐	☐	☐	☐
7. Our senior administration has a positive relationship with the teachers' association.	☐	☐	☐	☐	☐
8. Our senior administration has a positive relationship with parent groups.	☐	☐	☐	☐	☐
9. Our senior administration has a positive relationship with the principals' and vice-principals' association.	☐	☐	☐	☐	☐
10. Our senior administration has a positive relationship with labor unions.	☐	☐	☐	☐	☐
11. Our senior administration has a positive relationship with student groups.	☐	☐	☐	☐	☐

7.2 District Communicates Mission and Goals

12. Our district ensures public accessibility to its strategic plan.	☐	☐	☐	☐	☐
13. I have access to the district's strategic plan.	☐	☐	☐	☐	☐
14. District personnel inform the public of district goals and plans through public forums (e.g., service clubs).	☐	☐	☐	☐	☐
15. The public has been given avenues for authentic input into district decisions.	☐	☐	☐	☐	☐
16. The district actively elicits positive media coverage.	☐	☐	☐	☐	☐

References

Argyris, C., & Schön, D. (1978). *Organizational learning: A theory of action perspective.* Reading, MA.: Addison-Wesley.

Ball, D. L. (1990). Reflections and deflections of policy: The case of Carol Turner. *Educational Evaluation and Policy Analysis, 12*(3), 263-277.

Bandura, A. (1986). *Social foundations of thought and action.* Englewood Cliffs, NJ: Prentice Hall.

Banner, D. K., & Gagne, T. E. (1995). *Designing effective organizations: Traditional and transformational views.* Thousand Oaks, CA: Sage.

Barr, R., & Dreeben, R. (1983). *How schools work.* Chicago: University of Chicago Press.

Beck, L. G., & Foster, W. (1999). Administration and community: Considering challenges, exploring possibilities. In J. Murphy & K. S. Louis (Eds.), *Handbook of research on educational administration, second edition* (pp. 337-358). San Francisco: Jossey-Bass.

Bennis, W., & Nanus, B. (1985). *Leaders: The strategies for taking charge.* New York: Harper & Row.

Bereiter, C., & Scardamalia, M. (1994). *Surpassing ourselves: An inquiry into the nature and implications of expertise.* Chicago: Open Court.

Bloom, B. S. (1981). *All our children learning.* New York: McGraw-Hill.

Bolman, L. G., & Deal, T. E. (1991). *Reframing organizations.* San Francisco: Jossey-Bass.

British Columbia Ministry of Education. (1989). *Year 2000: A curriculum and assessment framework for the future.* Victoria, BC: Ministry of Education.

Brophy, J., & Good, T. (1986). Teacher behavior and student achievement. In M. Wittrock (Ed.), *Handbook of research on teaching, third edition* (pp. 328-375). New York: Macmillan.

Bryk, A. S., & Hermanson, K. L. (1993). Educational indicator systems: Observations on their structure, interpretation and use. In L. Darling-Hammond (Ed.), *Review of research in education* (Vol. 19, pp. 451-484). Washington, DC: American Educational Research Association.

Centra, J. A., & Potter, D. A. (1980). School and teacher effects: An interrelational model. *Review of Educational Research, 50*(2), 273-291.

Cohen, D. K., McLaughlin, M. W., & Talbert, J. E. (Eds.). (1993). *Teaching for understanding: Challenges for policy and practice*. San Francisco: Jossey-Bass.

Coleman, J. (1987). Families and schools. *Educational Researcher, 16*(6), 32-38.

Coleman, J. (1966). *Equality of educational opportunity*. Washington, DC: Government Printing Office.

Coleman, P., & LaRocque, L. (1991). *Struggling to be good enough*. London: Falmer Press.

Conley, S. (1991). Review of research on teacher participation in school decision making. In *Review of research in education, 17*. Washington, DC: American Educational Research Association.

Cousins, B., & Leithwood, K. (1986). Current empirical research on evaluation utilization. *Review of Educational Research, 56*(3), 331-364.

Cousins, B., & Leithwood, K. (1993). Enhancing knowledge utilization as a strategy for school improvement. *Knowledge: Creation, Diffusion, Utilization, 14*(3), 305-333.

Crowson, R. L. (1992). *School-community relations under reform*. Berkeley, CA: McCutchan.

Daft, R. L. (1989). *Organization theory and design* (3rd ed.). New York: West.

Darling-Hammond, L. (1993, June). Reframing the school reform agenda. *Phi Delta Kappan,* pp. 753-761.

Deal, T., & Peterson, K. (1990). *The principal's role in shaping school culture*. Washington, DC: U.S. Department of Education.

Deutschman, A. (1992). Why children should learn about work. *Fortune, 126*(3), 86-89.

Driscoll, M. E., & Kerchner, C. T. (1999). The implications of social capital for schools, communities, and cities: Educational administration as if a sense of place mattered. In J. Murphy & K. S. Louis (Eds.), *Handbook of research on educational administration, second edition* (pp. 385-404). San Francisco: Jossey-Bass.

Duignan, P. (1988). Reflective management: The key to quality leadership. *International Journal of Educational Management, 2*(2), 3-12.

Duke, D. (1986). The aesthetics of leadership. *Educational Administration Quarterly, 22*(1), 7-27.

Dunlap, D. N., & Goldman, P. (1991). Rethinking power in schools. *Educational Administration Quarterly, 27*(1), 5-29.

Faure, E., Herrera, F., Kaddoura, A., Lopes, H., Petrovsky, A., Rahnema, M., & Ward, F. C. (1973). *Learning to be: The world of education today and tomorrow*. Paris: UNESCO.

Fieman-Nemser, S., & Floden, R. E. (1986). The cultures of teaching. In M. Wittrock (Ed.), *Handbook of research on teaching* (pp. 505-526). New York: Macmillan.

Finn, J. (1989). Withdrawing from school. *Review of Educational Research, 59*(2), 117-143.

Finn, J., & Cox, D. (1992). Participation and withdrawal among fourth-grade pupils. *American Educational Research Journal, 29*(1), 141-162.

Fiol, C. M., & Lyles, M. (1985). Organizational learning. *Academy of Management Review, 10*, 803-813.

FitzGibbon, C. T. (1987). *How to analyze data*. Newbury Park, CA: Sage.

Fowler, F. J. (1988). *Survey research methods*. Newbury Park, CA: Sage.

Fowler, W. J., & Walberg, H. (1991). School size, characteristics and outcomes. *Educational Evaluation and Policy Analysis, 13*(2), 189-202.

Fraser, B. J., Walberg, H. J., Welch, W. W., & Hattie, J. A. (1987). Contextual and transactional influences on science outcomes. *International Journal of Educational Research, 11*(2), 165-185.

Fullan, M. (1991). *The new meaning of educational change*. New York: Teachers College Press.

Galbraith, J. (1977). *Organization design*. London: Addison-Wesley.

Gamoran, A. (1987). Organization, instruction and the effects of ability grouping. *Review of Educational Research, 57*(3), 341-346.

Gamoran, A., & Berends, M. (1987). The affects of stratification on secondary schools. *Review of Educational Research, 57*(4), 415-436.

Glasman, N., & Binianimov, I. (1981). Input-output analyses of schools. *Review of Educational Research, 51*(4), 509-539.

Gross, N., Giacquinta, J. B., & Bernstein, M. (1971). *Implementing organizational innovations*. New York: Basic Books.

Grossman, P., Wilson, S., & Shulman, L. (1989). Teachers of substance: Subject matter knowledge for teaching. In M. Reynolds (Ed.), *Knowledge base for the beginning teacher* (pp. 23-37). Oxford: Pergamon.

Haller, E. J. (1992). High school size and student indiscipline: Another aspect of the school consolidation issue. *Educational Evaluation and Policy Analysis, 14*(2), 145-156.

Hamilton, D. N. (1991). *The meaning in planning: An interpretive study of organizational planning in a school board.* Unpublished doctoral dissertation, University of Toronto.

Hannaway, J., & Talbert, J. E. (1993). Bringing context into effective schools research: Urban-suburban differences, *Educational Administration Quarterly, 29*(2), 164-186.

Hanushek, E. A. (1997). Outcomes, incentives, and beliefs: Reflections on analysis of the economics of schools. *Educational Evaluation and Policy Analysis, 19*(4), 301-308.

Hargreaves, A., & Macmillan, R. (1991, April). *Balkanized secondary schools and the malaise of modernity.* Paper presented at the annual meeting of the American Educational Research Association, San Francisco.

Hedberg, B. (1981). How organizations learn and unlearn. In P. C. Nystrom & W. H. Starbuck (Eds.). *Handbook of organizational design: Volume 1. Adapting organizations to their environments.* New York: Oxford University Press.

Henerson, M. E. (1987). *How to measure attitudes.* Newbury Park, CA: Sage.

Hunt, J. G. (1991). *Leadership: A new synthesis.* Newbury Park, CA: Sage.

Inbar, D. E. (1993). Educational planning: The transformation of symbols, frames of reference and behavior. *Educational Policy, 7*(2), 166-183.

Joyce, B., & Weil, M. (1972). *Models of teaching.* Englewood Cliffs, NJ: Prentice Hall.

Kagan, D. (1988). Teaching as clinical problem solving: A critical examination of the analogy and its implications. *Review of Educational Research, 58*(4), 482-505.

Kotter, J. P., & Heskett, J. L. (1992). *Corporate culture and performance.* New York: Free Press.

Kulik, C., & Kulik, J. (1982). Effects of ability grouping on secondary school students: A meta-analysis of evaluation findings. *American Educational Research Journal, 19*(3), 415-428.

Lareau, A. (1989). Family-school relationships: A view from the classroom. *Educational Policy, 3*(3), 245-289.

Lee, V. E., & Smith, J. B. (1997). High school size: Which works best and for whom? *Educational Evaluation and Policy Analysis, 19*(3), 205-227.

Leinhardt, G. (1992). What research tells us about teaching. *Educational Leadership, 49*(7), 20-25.

Leithwood, K. (1992). The move toward transformational leadership. *Educational Leadership, 49*(5), 8-12.

Leithwood, K. (1994). Leadership for school restructuring. *Educational Administration Quarterly, 30*(4), 498-518.

Leithwood, K. (Ed.). (1995). *Effective school district leadership: Transforming politics into education.* Albany, NY: SUNY Press.

Leithwood, K. (Ed.). (2000). *Understanding schools as intelligent systems.* London: JAI.

Leithwood, K., & Jantzi, D. (1990). Transformational leadership: How principals can help reform school cultures. *School Effectiveness and School Improvement, 1*(4), 249-280.

Leithwood, K., & Jantzi, D. (1999). The relative effects of principal and teacher sources of leadership on student engagement with school. *Educational Administration Quarterly, 35* (Suppl.), 679-706.

Leithwood, K., Cousins, B., Gérin-Lajoie, D., Jantzi, D., Joong, P., & Lévy, L. (1993). *Years of transition, times for change: Volume 2. Explaining variations in progress.* Toronto: Ontario Ministry of Education, final report of research.

Leithwood, K., Dart, B., Jantzi, D., & Steinbach, R. (1993). *Fostering organizational learning: A study of British Columbia's intermediate development site initiatives.* Victoria: British Columbia Ministry of Education, final research report.

Leithwood, K., & Joong, P. (1993). School-community relationships. In A. Hargreaves, K. Leithwood, D. Gérin-Lajoie, D. Thiessen, & B. Cousins, *Exemplary practices in the transition years: A review of research and theory.* Toronto: OISE, Report prepared for the Ontario Ministry of Education.

Leithwood, K., & Louis, K.S. (Eds.). (1998). *Organizational learning in schools.* The Netherlands: Swets & Zeitlinger.

Leithwood, K., Dart, B., Jantzi, D., & Steinbach, R. (1991). *Building commitment for change: A focus on school leadership.* Toronto: OISE, Report prepared for the British Columbia Ministry of Education.

Leithwood, K., Jantzi, D., & Steinbach, R. (1999). *Changing leadership for changing times*. Buckingham, UK: Open University Press.

Leithwood, K., Jantzi, D., Silins, H., & Dart, B. (1992, January). *Transformational leadership and school restructuring*. Paper presented at the International Congress on School Effectiveness and Improvement, Victoria, British Columbia.

Levitt, B., & March, J. G. (1988). Organizational learning. *Annual Review of Sociology, 14*, 319-340.

Linehan, M. F. (1992). Children who are homeless: Educational strategies for school personnel. *Phi Delta Kappan, 74*(1), 61-66.

Little, J. (1982). Norms of collegiality and experimentation: Workplace conditions of school sucess. *American Educational Research Journal, 19*, 325-340.

Lloyd, D. (1978). Prediction of school failure from third-grade data. *Educational and Psychological Measurement, 38*, 1193-1200.

Lortie, D. C. (1975). *Schoolteacher:A sociological study*. Chicago: University of Chicago Press.

Louis, K. S., & Kruse, S. (1998). Creating community in reform: Images of organizational learning in inner-city schools. In K. Leithwood, & K. S. Louis (Eds.), *Organizational learning in schools* (pp. 17-45). The Netherlands: Swets & Zeitlinger.

Madaus, G., & Tan, A. (1993). The growth of assessment. In G. Cawelti (Ed.), *Challenges and achievements of American education: The 1993 ASCD yearbook*. Alexandria, VA: ASCD.

Madden, N. A., Slavin, R. E., Karweit, N., Dolan, L., & Wasik, B. A. (1993). Success for all: Longitudinal effects of a restructuring program for inner-city elementary schools. *American Educational Research Journal, 30*(1), 123-148.

March, J., & Simon, H. (1958). *Organizations*. New York: John Wiley.

Maslow, A. (1970). *Motivation and personality* (2nd ed.). New York: Harper & Row.

Massie, J. (1965). Management theory. In J. March (Ed.), *Handbook of organizations*. Chicago: Rand McNally.

McLaughlin, M. (1992). How district communities do and do not foster teacher pride. *Educational Leadership, 50*(1), 33-35.

McNeil, D., & Freiberger, P. (1993). *Fuzzy logic: The discovery of a revolutionary computer technology—and how it is changing our world*. New York: Simon & Schuster.

Mintzberg, H. (1993). *The rise and fall of strategic planning*. New York: Free Press.

Monk, D. H. (1984). The conception of size and the internal allocation of school district resources. *Educational Administration Quarterly, 20*(1), 39-67.

Murnane, R., & Levy, F. (1996). Teaching to new standards. In S. H. Fuhrman & J. O'Day (Eds.), *Rewards and reform: Creating educational incentives that work* (pp. 257-293). San Francisco: Jossey-Bass.

Murphy, J. (1991). *Restructuring schools*. New York: Teachers College Press.

Musella, D., & Davis, J. (1991). Assessing organizational culture: Implications for leaders of organizational change. In K. Leithwood & D. Musella (Eds.), *Understanding school system administration* (pp. 287-305). London: Falmer.

Naisbitt, J., & Aburdene, P. (1985). *Reinventing the corporation*. New York: Warner Publications.

National Center for Education Statistics. (1991). *Education counts*. Washington, DC: U.S. Office of Education.

Newell, A., & Simon, H. (1972). *Human problem solving*. Englewood Cliffs, NJ: Prentice Hall.

Newman, Cardinal J. H. (1961). *On the scope and nature of university education*. London: J. M. Dent & Sons Ltd.

Oakes, J. (1986). *Educational indicators: A guide for policymakers*. New Brunswick, NJ: Center for Policy Research in Education, Rutgers University.

Oakes, J. (1989). What educational indicators? The case for assessing the school context. *Educational Evaluation and Policy Analysis, 11*(2), 181-199.

Odden, A. (1996). Incentives, school organization, and teacher compensation. In S. H. Fuhrman & J. O'Day (Eds.), *Rewards and reform: Creating educational incentives that work* (pp. 226-256). San Francisco: Jossey-Bass.

Orr, M. T. (1989). *Keeping students in school*. San Francisco: Jossey-Bass.

Perkins, D. (1992). *Smart schools: From training memories to educating minds*. New York: Free Press.

Peterson, P. (1979). Direct instruction reconsidered. In P. Peterson & H. Walberg (Eds.), *Research on teaching* (pp. 57-69). Berkeley: McCutchan.

Podsakoff, P. M., MacKenzie, S. B., Moorman, R. H., & Fetter, R. (1990). Transformational leader behaviors and their effects on followers' trust in leader, satisfaction, and organizational citizenship behaviors. *Leadership Quarterly, 1*(2), 107-142.

Posner, M. (Ed.). (1990). *Foundations of cognitive science.* Cambridge: MIT Press.

Prawat, R. S., & Peterson, P. L. (1999). Social constructivist views of learning. In J. Murphy & K. S. Louis (Eds.), *Handbook of research on educational administration, second edition* (pp. 203-226). San Francisco: Jossey-Bass.

Radwanski, G. (1987). *Ontario study of the relevance of education and the issue of dropouts.* Toronto: Ontario Ministry of Education.

Reynolds, M. C. (Ed.). (1989). *Knowledge base for the beginning teacher.* Oxford, UK: Pergamon.

Roberts, N. (1985). Transforming leadership: A process of collective action. *Human Relations, 38*(11), 1023-1046.

Rosenholtz, S. (1989). *Teachers' workplace.* New York: Longmans.

Rosenshine, B. (1979). Content, time and direct instruction. In P. Peterson & H. Walberg (Eds.), *Research on teaching* (pp. 28-56). Berkeley: McCutchan.

Rumberger, R. W. (1983). Dropping out of high school: The influence of race, sex and family background. *American Educational Research Journal, 20,* 199-220.

Rumberger, R. W. (1987). High school dropouts: A review of issues and evidence. *Review of Educational Research, 57*(2), 101-121.

Rutter, M., Maugham, B., Mortimore, P., & Outston, J. (1979). *Fifteen thousand hours: Secondary schools and their effects on students.* Cambridge, MA: Harvard University Press.

Sarason, S. (1990). *The predictable failure of educational reform.* San Francisco: Jossey-Bass.

Schön, D. (1987). *Educating the reflective practitioner.* San Francisco: Jossey-Bass.

Schwartz, P. (1991). *The art of the long view.* New York: Doubleday.

Scott-Jones, P. (1984). Family influences on cognitive development and school achievement. In E. Gordon (Ed.), *Review of research in education, 11.* Washington, DC: American Educational Research Association.

Selden, R. (1990). Developing educational indicators: A state-national perspective. *International Journal of Educational Research, 14,* 383-393.

Senge, P. M. (1990). *The fifth discipline: The art and practice of the learning organization*. London: Doubleday.

Sergiovanni, T. (1994). *Building community in schools*. San Francisco: Jossey-Bass.

Sheerens, J. (1990). School effectiveness research and the development of process indicators of school functioning. *School Effectiveness and School Improvement, 1*(1), 61-80.

Sieber, S. (1981). *Fatal remedies: The ironies of social intervention*. New York: Plenum.

Sitkin, S. B. (1992). Learning through failure: The strategy of small losses. In B. M. Staw & L. L. Cummings (Eds.), *Research in organizational behavior, Vol. 14*. London: JAI.

Slavin, R. (1987). Ability grouping and student achievement in elementary schools: A best-evidence synthesis. *Review of Educational Research, 57*(3), 337-350.

Snydor, J., & Ebmeier, H. (1992). Empirical linkages among principal behaviors and intermediate outcomes: Implications for principal education. *Peabody Journal of Education, 68*(1), 75-107.

Stringfield, S., & Herman, R. (1996). Assessment of the state of school effectiveness research in the United States of America. *School Effectiveness and School Improvement, 7*(2), 159-180.

Walberg, H. (1984). Improving the productivity of America's schools. *Educational Leadership, 40*, 19-27.

Walberg, H. (1986). Synthesis of research on teaching. In M. Wittrock (Ed.), *Handbook of research on teaching: 3rd edition* (pp. 214-229). New York: Macmillan.

Walford, G. (1993). The real lessons in school reform from Britain. *Educational Policy, 7*(2), 212-222.

Weick, K. E., & Bougon, M. G. (1986). Organizations as cognitive maps: Charting ways to success and failure. In H. Sims, D. Gioia, & Associates (Eds.), *The thinking organization* (pp. 102-135). San Francisco: Jossey-Bass.

Weinstein, C. S. (1979). The physical environment of the school. *Review of Educational Research, 49*(4), 577-610.

Windham, D. M. (1987). Effective indicators in economic analysis of educational activities. *International Journal of Educational Research, 12*, 593-647.

Author Index

Subject Index